How to Use This Book

A Variety of Presentations

1. Make overhead transparencies of the lessons. Present each lesson as an oral activity with the entire class. Write answers and make corrections using an erasable marker.

    As the class becomes more familiar with *Daily Word Problems,* have students mark their answers first and then check them against correct responses marked on the transparency.

2. Reproduce the problems for individuals or partners to work on independently. Check answers as a group, using an overhead transparency to model the solutions' strategies. (Use these pages as independent practice only after much group experience with the lessons.)

3. Occasionally you may want to reproduce problems as a test to see how individuals are progressing in their acquisition of skills.

Important Considerations

1. Allow students to use whatever tools they need to solve problems. Some students will choose to use manipulatives, while others will want to make drawings. Calculators may be made available to allow students to focus on the solution process.

2. It is important that students share their solutions. Modeling a variety of problem-solving techniques makes students aware that there are different paths to the correct answer. Don't scrimp on the amount of time allowed for discussing how solutions were reached.

3. Teach students to follow problem-solving strategies:
   - Read the problem carefully more than one time. Think about it as you read.
   - Mark the important information in the problem.
       What question does the problem ask?
       What words will help you know how to solve the problem (*in all, left, how many more,* etc.)?
       What facts will help you answer the question? (Cross out facts that are NOT needed.)
   - Think about what you need to do to solve the problem (add, subtract, multiply, or divide).
   - Solve the problem. Does your answer make sense?
   - Check your answer.

Matrix Logic Puzzles

The Friday problems for weeks 1, 5, 8, 12, 15, 18, 21, 24, 31, 34, and 36 are matrix logic puzzles. Here are some guidelines for helping students solve this type of logic puzzle:

- Read all the clues. Find clues that give a definite *Yes* or *No.* (For example: John plays the clarinet. Sally does not play the flute.) Mark boxes with X (for no) or *Yes.*
- When you mark a box *Yes,* mark Xs in all the other boxes in that row and in the column above and below the X.
- Find clues that give information, but not enough to tell you how to mark the boxes. Make notes in the boxes for later use.
- Go over each clue again. Look for clues that fit together to give enough information to make a box *Yes* or X (no).

Scope and Sequence–Grade 6

Week	1	2	3	4	5	6	7	8	9	10	11	12	13	14	15	16	17	18	19	20	21	22	23	24	25	26	27	28	29	30	31	32	33	34	35	36
Addition & Subtraction	•	•	•	•	•	•	•			•					•	•	•	•	•	•	•	•	•	•	•	•	•	•			•	•		•	•	•
1-, 2- & 3-Digit Multiplication		•	•		•	•		•	•	•	•	•	•	•	•				•	•	•	•	•	•	•	•	•	•	•			•	•	•	•	•
1-Digit Divisors				•	•							•				•			•	•			•					•	•		•				•	
2- & 3-Digit Divisors			•				•	•			•						•									•	•	•								
Fractions		•		•	•	•	•	•	•		•									•		•	•			•	•					•	•			•
Decimals	•		•						•				•	•		•						•	•	•						•	•	•			•	
Percents							•			•															•		•		•	•					•	•
Time	•					•					•				•		•				•			•		•				•					•	
Money	•	•	•		•	•	•	•	•	•	•	•	•	•	•	•		•	•	•	•	•		•	•	•	•	•		•	•	•	•		•	•
Linear Measurement	•							•			•		•	•			•			•			•						•					•		
Weight and Capacity		•	•	•		•	•	•				•			•							•	•								•			•		
Interpreting Graphs				•					•		•	•	•			•			•	•				•	•				•			•		•		
Geometry									•									•				•							•	•					•	
Probability					•		•		•		•							•					•			•		•	•	•						
Logic					•										•	•					•										•				•	•
Averages, Mode, Range			•		•			•							•		•			•		•		•	•	•	•	•	•			•	•	•		
Area, Perimeter, & Volume														•									•											•		
Integers													•			•							•					•								•

Daily Word Problems • EMC 3006

Daily Word Problems

Monday-Week 1

Swim Meet

There were 16 schools at the regional swim meet. An average of 14 swimmers were on each school team. How many swimmers were at the swim meet?

Name:

Work Space:

Answer:

_____

Daily Word Problems

Tuesday-Week 1

Swim Meet

When the swimmers first arrived at the pool, the temperature of the water was only 72.5 degrees. By the time the first race started, the temperature had gone up 5.6 degrees. What was the temperature of the water when the first race started?

Name:

Work Space:

Answer:

_____

Daily Word Problems

Wednesday-Week 1

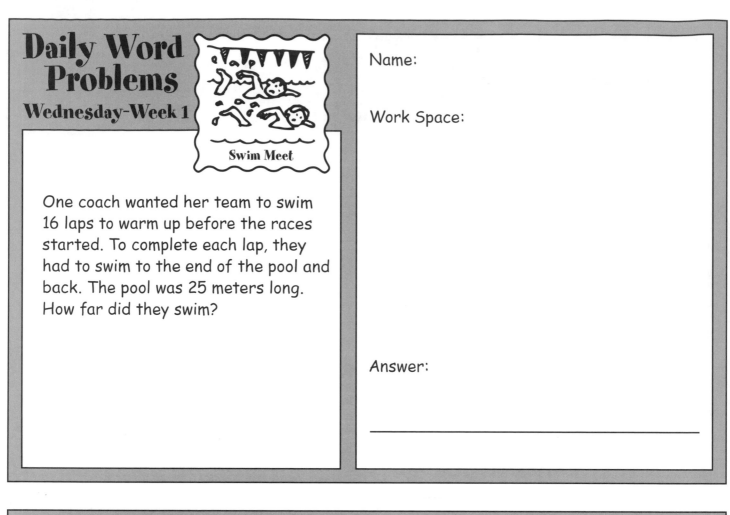

Swim Meet

One coach wanted her team to swim 16 laps to warm up before the races started. To complete each lap, they had to swim to the end of the pool and back. The pool was 25 meters long. How far did they swim?

Name:

Work Space:

Answer:

_____

Daily Word Problems

Thursday-Week 1

Swim Meet

Jessie finished the first race in 2 minutes 7 seconds. Tim finished 12 seconds faster than Jessie. Juan finished 8 seconds faster than Tim. How long did it take Juan to finish?

Name:

Work Space:

Answer:

_____

Daily Word Problems

Friday-Week 1

Swim Meet

Use the clues below to determine who placed first, second, third, fourth, and fifth in the 100-meter medley.

When you know that a name and a place do **not** go with each other, make an **X** under the place and across from the name. When you know that a name and place do go together, write YES in that box. You can then **X** that name and place for all others.

	First	Second	Third	Fourth	Fifth
Susan					
Janice					
Maria					
Jennifer					
Emily					

Clues:

1. Susan finished the race in second place.

2. The swimmers who placed first and fourth have names that start with the same letter.

3. Maria finished immediately after Janice.

4. Jennifer finished before Emily.

Daily Word Problems

Monday-Week 2

Garage Sale

The Martinez family started their garage sale one half hour after the Smith family. The Smith family started their garage sale one hour before the Carson family, who started theirs at 8:30 a.m. At what time did the Martinez family start their garage sale?

Name:

Work Space:

Answer:

Daily Word Problems

Tuesday-Week 2

Garage Sale

Shirley picked out a kite for $3.50. If she gave the family a ten-dollar bill, what is the fewest number of bills and coins that she could receive as change?

Name:

Work Space:

Answer:

Daily Word Problems

Wednesday-Week 2

GARAGE SALE TODAY

Garage Sale

At the end of the day, the Dirk family announced that all items were half price. If the sticker on a jacket read $3.00, how much would it sell for?

Name:

Work Space:

Answer:

_____

Daily Word Problems

Thursday-Week 2

GARAGE SALE TODAY

Garage Sale

Alex and his friend Kim made a one-gallon pitcher of lemonade because it was so hot. They drank 5 glasses that each held 2 cups of lemonade. How much lemonade was left in the pitcher? Express the answer in two different ways. (Hint: There are 4 cups in 1 quart and 4 quarts in 1 gallon.)

Name:

Work Space:

Answer:

_____

_____

Daily Word Problems

Friday-Week 2

Garage Sale

Nancy's family recorded the amounts of money that were collected at their garage sale.

Person	Amounts of Money Collected
Nancy	45¢, $1, 75¢, $1.25
John	$2, $2, $1.50, 25¢
Susan	$5
Scott	$3, $1.75, 30¢
Judy	90¢, 35¢, 75¢, 25¢, 10¢, 75¢

- What was the average amount of money that the five people in Nancy's family collected during the garage sale?

_____

Daily Word Problems

Monday-Week 3

Zoo Trip

The sixth-grade class from Franklin Middle School is going to the zoo on a field trip. There are 270 students who want to go on the field trip. If the school requires one adult for every 15 students, how many adults will be needed for the field trip?

Name:

Work Space:

Answer:

_____

Daily Word Problems

Tuesday-Week 3

Zoo Trip

Sharon wants to sit in the back seat of the bus on the trip to the zoo. The back seat is the full width of the bus and seats five students. If Sharon selects her place on the seat at random, what is the probability that she will sit at either end by a window?

Name:

Work Space:

Answer:

_____

Daily Word Problems

Wednesday-Week 3

Zoo Trip

The regular price for admission to the zoo is $7.00. There is a 25% discount off the price of each ticket for school groups. How much will each ticket cost with the discount?

Name:

Work Space:

Answer:

_____

Daily Word Problems

Thursday-Week 3

Zoo Trip

The male elephant at the zoo weighs about 7 tons. How many pounds does that elephant weigh? (Hint: 1 ton equals 2,000 pounds.)

Name:

Work Space:

Answer:

_____

Daily Word Problems

Name:

Zoo Trip

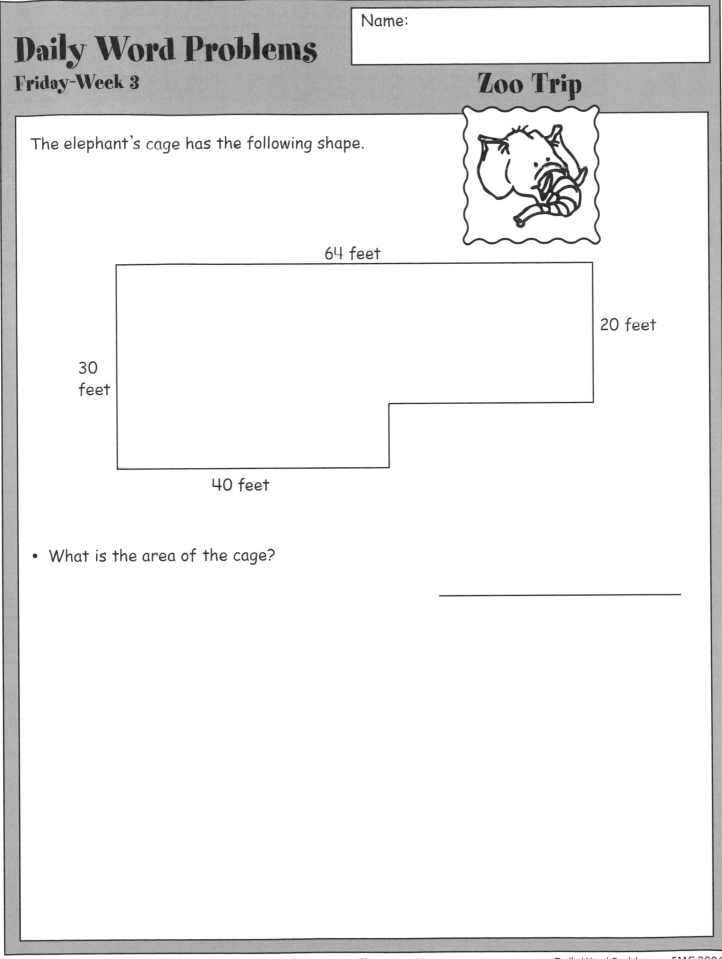

The elephant's cage has the following shape.

64 feet

20 feet

30 feet

40 feet

• What is the area of the cage?

_____

Daily Word Problems

Monday—Week 4

Pet Store

The pet store has 8 rabbits for sale. Each morning the owner feeds the rabbits a total of 2 cups of pellets. If each rabbit receives the same amount of pellets, how much does each rabbit receive?

Name:

Work Space:

Answer:

_____

Daily Word Problems

Tuesday—Week 4

Pet Store

One of the fish tanks on display at the pet store is shaped like an octagonal prism. How many rectangles of glass are around the edge of the fish tank?

Name:

Work Space:

Answer:

_____

Daily Word Problems

Wednesday-Week 4

Pet Store

On Monday there were 92 fish in the fish tank. On Tuesday 4 fish were sold, on Wednesday 1 fish was sold, on Thursday 4 fish were added to the tank, and on Friday 3 fish were sold. How many fish were in the fish tank at the end of the week?

Name:

Work Space:

Answer:

_____

Daily Word Problems

Thursday-Week 4

Pet Store

Helen counts the fish in each of the fish tanks and finds the following totals: 57, 119, 29, 23, and 48. What is the total number of fish?

Name:

Work Space:

Answer:

_____

Daily Word Problems

Name:

Pet Store

The graph below shows the income and expenses for four weeks at the pet store.

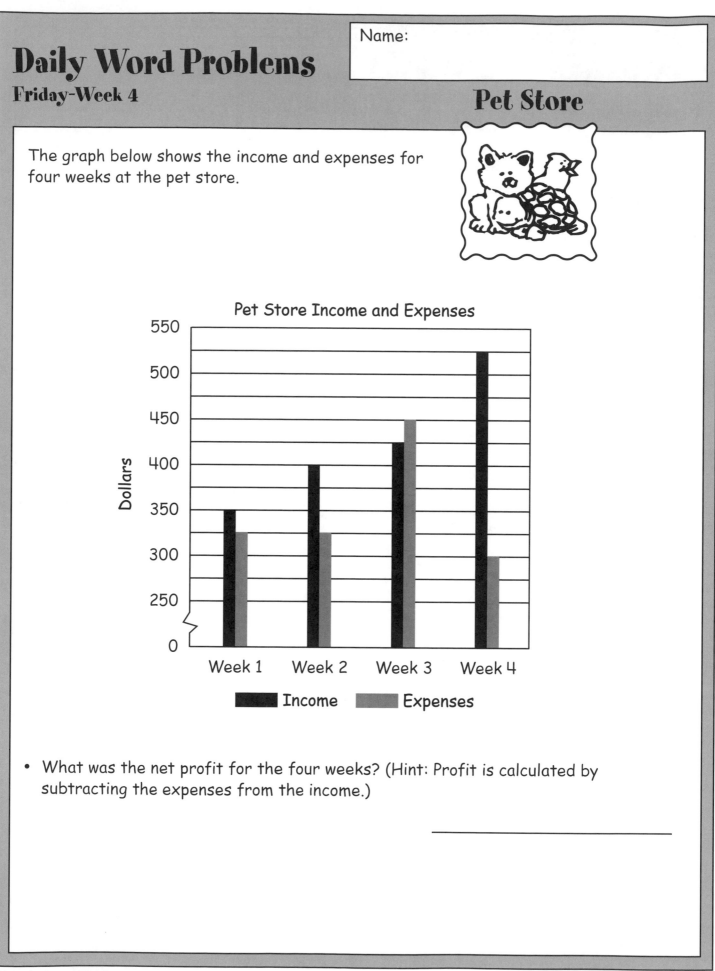

Pet Store Income and Expenses

Dollars

550
500
450
400
350
300
250
0

Week 1   Week 2   Week 3   Week 4

■ Income   ■ Expenses

- What was the net profit for the four weeks? (Hint: Profit is calculated by subtracting the expenses from the income.)

_____

Daily Word Problems

Monday-Week 5

Concert

The tickets for the concert are selling for $12.00. Juanita is going to the concert with a group of 25 people. There is a discount of $\frac{1}{8}$ off each ticket for groups. How much will each ticket cost after the discount?

Name:

Work Space:

Answer:

_____

Daily Word Problems

Tuesday-Week 5

Concert

There were three concerts in Lakeside. The first concert had 953 people in attendance. The second and third concerts each had a full house of 1,100. What was the average number of people at the three concerts?

Name:

Work Space:

Answer:

_____

Daily Word Problems

Wednesday-Week 5

Concert

The stage lights for the concert were suspended on a metal rack constructed in three sections. The bottom section was 12 feet tall. The section above that was 3 yards tall. The top section was only 35 inches tall. How tall was the entire metal rack in feet and inches?

Name:

Work Space:

Answer:

_____

Daily Word Problems

Thursday-Week 5

Concert

During intermission, Shari bought a soda for 79¢. If she paid with a one-dollar bill, what are three different combinations of coins that she could have received as change?

Name:

Work Space:

Answer:

_____

_____

_____

Daily Word Problems

Friday–Week 5

Concert

Use the clues below to determine what number seat each of these five students sat in for the concert.

Use the clues to help you fill in the seat numbers in the top row. When you know that a name and a seat number do **not** go with each other, make an X under the seat number and across from the name. When you know that a name and seat number do go together, write YES in that box. You can then X that name and seat number for all others.

Daniel					
Dwight					
Janet					
Harry					
Suzy					

Clues:

1. The seats were numbered consecutively, starting with 10 and ending with seat number 14.

2. Daniel and Dwight sat in the odd-numbered seats.

3. Janet's seat number is three more than Daniel's seat number.

4. Harry's seat number is two less than Suzy's seat number.

Daily Word Problems

Monday-Week 6

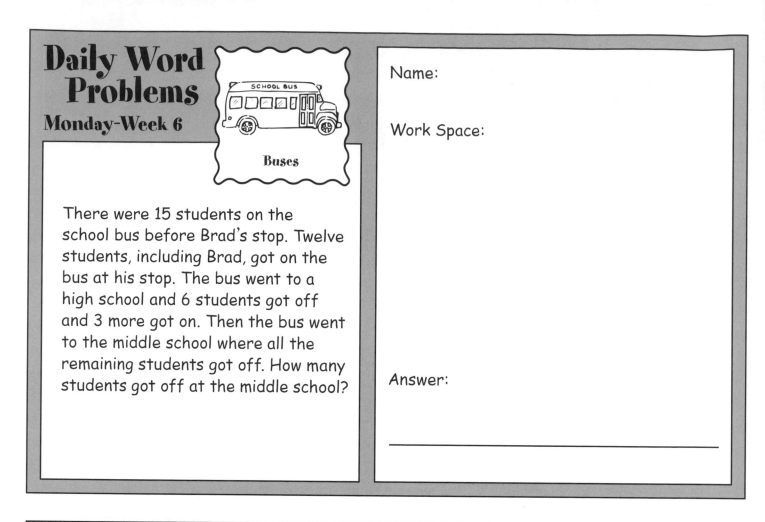

Buses

There were 15 students on the school bus before Brad's stop. Twelve students, including Brad, got on the bus at his stop. The bus went to a high school and 6 students got off and 3 more got on. Then the bus went to the middle school where all the remaining students got off. How many students got off at the middle school?

Name:

Work Space:

Answer:

Daily Word Problems

Tuesday-Week 6

SCHOOL BUS

Buses

Jennifer left her house at 6:45 a.m. It took her 8 minutes 45 seconds to walk to the bus stop. She waited $3\frac{3}{4}$ minutes for the bus and then rode the bus $7\frac{1}{2}$ minutes to her school. At what time did she arrive at school?

Name:

Work Space:

Answer:

Daily Word Problems

Wednesday-Week 6

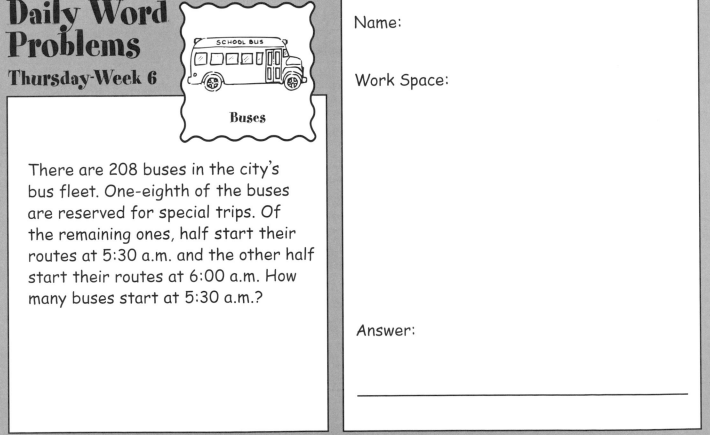

Buses

An annual pass for the city bus costs $26. Paul and his three friends each bought an annual pass. How much money did they pay in all for the passes?

Name:

Work Space:

Answer:

_____

Daily Word Problems

Thursday-Week 6

Buses

There are 208 buses in the city's bus fleet. One-eighth of the buses are reserved for special trips. Of the remaining ones, half start their routes at 5:30 a.m. and the other half start their routes at 6:00 a.m. How many buses start at 5:30 a.m.?

Name:

Work Space:

Answer:

_____

Daily Word Problems

Name:

Buses

The map below shows several cities that buses pass through when they travel from Evans to Westview. The numbers represent the number of minutes it takes to travel each road.

Use the map to determine the **fastest** bus route from Evans to Westview. Write the names of the cities and the number of minutes it takes on that route on the lines below.

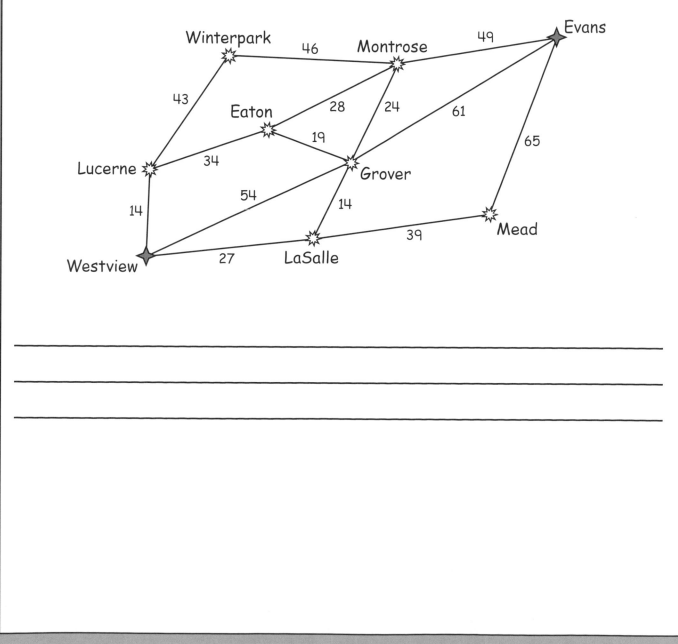

_____

_____

_____

Daily Word Problems • EMC 3006

Daily Word Problems

Monday-Week 7

Haircuts

There are 18 people who work at the Cut and Style Shop. They put all the tips they earn into a pot and equally divide the money at the end of each month. Last month the money in the pot totaled $2,232. How much did each person receive?

Name:

Work Space:

Answer:

_____

Daily Word Problems

Tuesday-Week 7

Haircuts

Each chair in the Cut and Style Shop can hold a maximum weight of 450 pounds. A large gentleman walked into the shop. He told his stylist that he weighed 75 pounds less than a quarter of a ton. By how many pounds is the gentleman over or under the maximum weight? (Hint: One ton equals 2,000 pounds.)

Name:

Work Space:

Answer:

_____

Daily Word Problems

Wednesday-Week 7

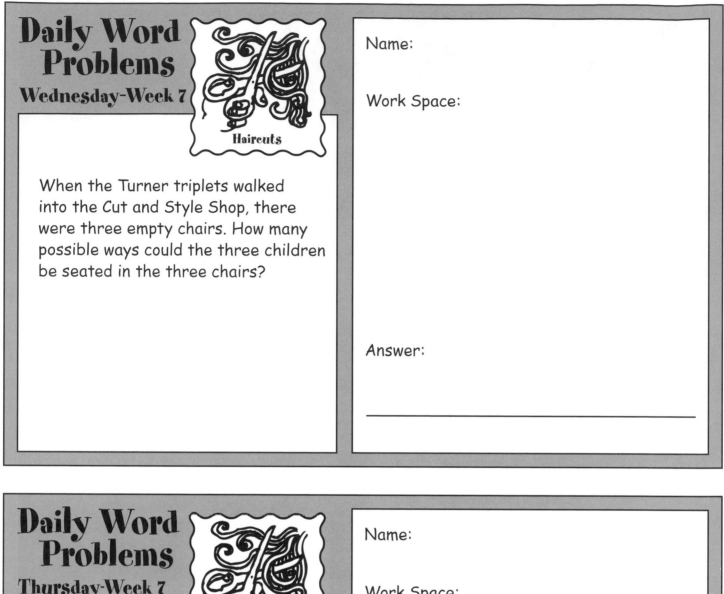

Haircuts

When the Turner triplets walked into the Cut and Style Shop, there were three empty chairs. How many possible ways could the three children be seated in the three chairs?

Name:

Work Space:

Answer:

_____

Daily Word Problems

Thursday-Week 7

Haircuts

Josie is getting her hair cut and styled. She wants to give a 20% tip to her stylist. If the haircut costs $15.00, how much tip should she give?

Name:

Work Space:

Answer:

_____

Daily Word Problems

Haircuts

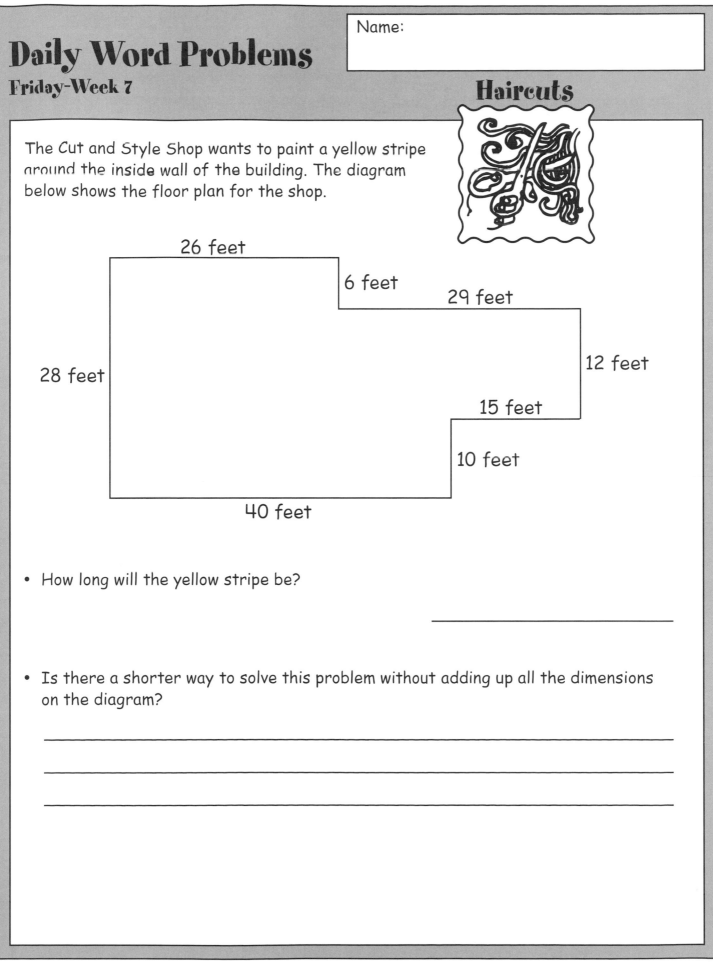

Name:

The Cut and Style Shop wants to paint a yellow stripe around the inside wall of the building. The diagram below shows the floor plan for the shop.

26 feet

6 feet

29 feet

28 feet

12 feet

15 feet

10 feet

40 feet

• How long will the yellow stripe be?

_____

• Is there a shorter way to solve this problem without adding up all the dimensions on the diagram?

_____

_____

_____

Daily Word Problems

Monday-Week 8

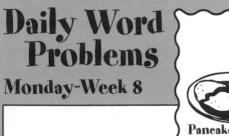

Pancake Breakfast

Name:

Work Space:

There are 36 tables set up for the annual pancake breakfast. Each table is 8 feet long. The students plan to cover each table with a paper tablecloth that extends an extra 4 inches over each end so they can tape it underneath. What is the total length of paper needed to cover all the tables?

Answer:

_____

Daily Word Problems

Tuesday-Week 8

Pancake Breakfast

Name:

Work Space:

The recipe for the pancake batter calls for $\frac{3}{4}$ cup of milk. The students want to make a batch of pancake batter that will quadruple the recipe. How much milk will they need in all?

Answer:

_____

Daily Word Problems

Wednesday-Week 8

Pancake Breakfast

The students had 2,500 forks at the pancake breakfast. There were four service stations. To evenly spread out the forks, how many forks were at each service station?

Name:

Work Space:

Answer:

_____

Daily Word Problems

Thursday-Week 8

Pancake Breakfast

There were seven serving lines at the annual pancake breakfast. The total number of people served at each of the seven lines were 126, 118, 127, 134, 98, 132, and 121. What was the median number of people served?

Name:

Work Space:

Answer:

_____

Daily Word Problems

Name:

Pancake Breakfast

At the pancake breakfast, there were four stations set up where people donated money toward new playground equipment. Use the clues below to determine how much money was donated at each of the four stations.

Use the clues to help you fill in the different amounts of money. When you know that a station and an amount of money do **not** go with each other, make an X under the amount of money and across from the station. When you know that a station and an amount of money do go together, write YES in that box. You can then X that station and amount of money for all others.

Station 1				
Station 2				
Station 3				
Station 4				

Clues:

1. Station 3 collected the most with $343.

2. The range of the money collected was $231.

3. Station 4 collected the least amount of money.

4. Station 2 collected $88 less than station 3.

5. Station 1 collected $94 more than station 4.

Daily Word Problems

Monday-Week 9

Grocery Store

Valeria had a coupon for one-third off her total bill at the local grocery store. She bought 2 six-packs of soda for $1.45 each, three bags of chips for $2.49 each, and a half-gallon of ice cream for $4.60. How much was Valeria's bill with the discount?

Name:

Work Space:

Answer:

_____

Daily Word Problems

Tuesday-Week 9

Grocery Store

In each variety pack of fruit juice, there are 3 boxes of apple juice, 2 boxes of grape juice, and 1 box of orange juice. In a display in the store, there are 16 cases of juice with 8 variety packs in each case. How many boxes of juice are in the display?

Name:

Work Space:

Answer:

_____

Daily Word Problems

Wednesday-Week 9

Grocery Store

Think about a cereal box. What geometric shape is a cereal box? What geometric shape is each of the faces of a cereal box?

Name:

Work Space:

Answer:

_____

_____

Daily Word Problems

Thursday-Week 9

Grocery Store

Jon is buying some candy for 19¢. He has only dimes, nickels, and pennies in his pocket. List **all** the different combinations of dimes, nickels, and pennies he could use to pay for the candy.

Name:

Answer:

Name:

Grocery Store

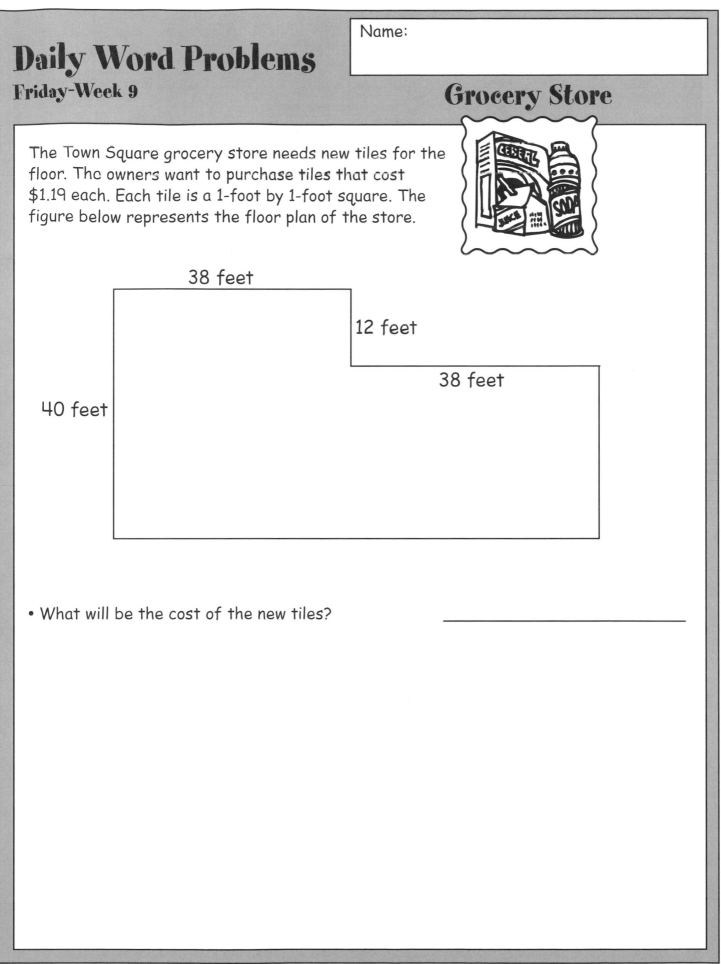

The Town Square grocery store needs new tiles for the floor. The owners want to purchase tiles that cost $1.19 each. Each tile is a 1-foot by 1-foot square. The figure below represents the floor plan of the store.

38 feet

12 feet

38 feet

40 feet

• What will be the cost of the new tiles? _____

Daily Word Problems

Monday-Week 10

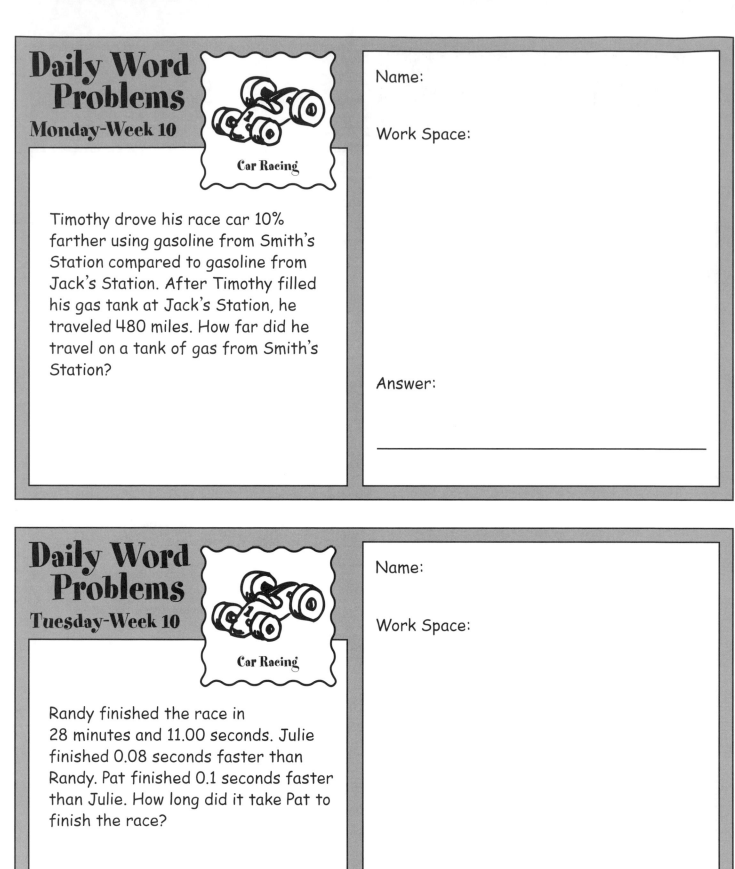

Car Racing

Timothy drove his race car 10% farther using gasoline from Smith's Station compared to gasoline from Jack's Station. After Timothy filled his gas tank at Jack's Station, he traveled 480 miles. How far did he travel on a tank of gas from Smith's Station?

Name:

Work Space:

Answer:

_____

Daily Word Problems

Tuesday-Week 10

Car Racing

Randy finished the race in 28 minutes and 11.00 seconds. Julie finished 0.08 seconds faster than Randy. Pat finished 0.1 seconds faster than Julie. How long did it take Pat to finish the race?

Name:

Work Space:

Answer:

_____

Daily Word Problems
Wednesday-Week 10

Car Racing

Trevor won several races last season. The following list shows the cash prizes he won at the races.

$7,000; $25,000; $6,500; $10,050; $650

What was Trevor's total winnings last season?

Name:

Work Space:

Answer:

_____

Daily Word Problems
Thursday-Week 10

Car Racing

The races had 3,832 people in attendance on Thursday, 4,295 people on Friday, and 4,783 people on Saturday. If the racetrack seats 5,000 people, how many empty seats were there in all for the three races?

Name:

Work Space:

Answer:

_____

Daily Word Problems

Friday-Week 10

Car Racing

Frenzy Cars tested five cars on a short track. The chart below shows the length of time each car took to complete the track once.

Car	Time
1	4 minutes 30 seconds
2	5 minutes 12 seconds
3	4 minutes 24 seconds
4	4 minutes 51 seconds
5	5 minutes 3 seconds

- What is the range of time for these five cars?

  _____

- What is the average length of time it took the five cars to go around the track one time?

  _____

Daily Word Problems

Monday-Week 11

Birthdays

Suzanne wants to take 12 friends to see a movie to celebrate her birthday. The tickets for the movie cost $6.50 each. How much money does she need for all of them?

Name:

Work Space:

Answer:

_____

Daily Word Problems

Tuesday-Week 11

Birthdays

Jim wants his birthday party to last for 3 hours and to be over at least 30 minutes before his bedtime. If his bedtime is at 9:00 p.m., what is the latest time he can start his birthday party?

Name:

Work Space:

Answer:

_____

Daily Word Problems

Wednesday-Week 11

Birthdays

At Kayleen's birthday party there will be eight kids including Kayleen. They will place each person's name in a hat. Without looking, they will draw one name out of the hat to see who will answer the door when the pizza deliverer arrives. What is the probability that Kayleen's name will be drawn?

Name:

Work Space:

Answer:

_____

Daily Word Problems

Thursday-Week 11

Birthdays

Julia took a jar of candy to school to share with her classmates for her birthday. There were 900 pieces of candy in the jar. The candy was divided equally among 28 students and the teacher. How many pieces of candy did each person receive? How many pieces of candy were left over?

Name:

Work Space:

Answer:

_____

_____

Birthdays

When Stephen's little brother finished his birthday dinner, he needed a bath. He closed the drain in the bathtub and turned on the water faucet at 6:00 p.m. The following graph represents the depth of the water in the bathtub from 6:00 p.m. until 6:20 p.m.

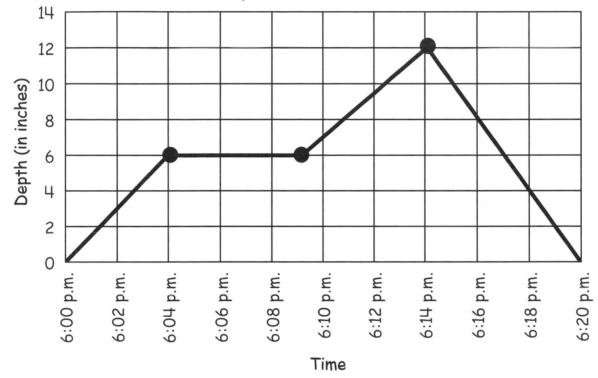

Depth of Water in Bathtub

Describe some possible reasons for the changes in water depth at each of the following times.

Time	Possible reason for change in water depth
6:00 p.m.	He closed the drain and turned on the water faucet.
6:04 p.m.	
6:09 p.m.	
6:14 p.m.	

Daily Word Problems

Monday-Week 12

Baking

Elliott is baking cookies. For one batch of cookies he needs $\frac{1}{4}$ cup of brown sugar and $1\frac{1}{2}$ cups of white sugar. If he doubles the recipe, how much brown sugar and white sugar will he need?

Name:

Work Space:

Answer:

_____

_____

Daily Word Problems

Tuesday-Week 12

Baking

There are 4 sticks in one pound of butter. Each stick is equal to 8 tablespoons or $\frac{1}{2}$ cup. The recipe that Samantha is making calls for $1\frac{1}{2}$ cups of butter. How many sticks of butter does she need? What is the weight of the butter she needs for her recipe?

Name:

Work Space:

Answer:

_____

_____

Daily Word Problems

Wednesday-Week 12

Baking

Jorge is baking cookies. The recipe makes 144 cookies. If Jorge and his 5 friends want to divide the cookies evenly, how many cookies will each person get?

Name:

Work Space:

Answer:

_____

Daily Word Problems

Thursday-Week 12

Baking

South Side Elementary School is having a bake sale to raise money for some new computers. They are selling pies for $5.00 each and cookies for $2.50 a dozen. Ivania wants to buy 3 pies and 2 dozen cookies. If she pays with a twenty-dollar bill, what change should she get back?

Name:

Work Space:

Answer:

_____

Daily Word Problems

Name:

Baking

Five people each volunteered to bake a different kind of pie for the school Teacher Appreciation Dinner. The five pies are pecan, peach, cherry, apple, and chocolate. Use the clues below to determine who baked each pie.

Use the clues to help you fill in the names of the people. When you know that a person and a pie do **not** go with each other, make an X under the pie and across from the person. When you know that a person and pie do go together, write YES in that box. You can then X that person and pie for all others.

	Pecan	Peach	Cherry	Apple	Chocolate

Clues:

1. The names of the five people are Bryan, Jose, Linda, Nan, and Victor.

2. Victor did not make a fruit pie.

3. Linda made either the peach pie or the chocolate pie.

4. Nan made either the cherry pie or the pecan pie.

5. Bryan made a pie that starts with the letter "p".

6. One of the boys made the peach pie.

Daily Word Problems

Monday–Week 13

Weather

At 6 a.m. the temperature was 26 degrees Fahrenheit. At noon a snowstorm started, which caused the temperature to drop 32 degrees. What was the temperature at noon?

Name:

Work Space:

Answer:

_____

Daily Word Problems

Tuesday–Week 13

Weather

Snow fell for 20% of the days in November. How many days in November did it snow? (Hint: There are 30 days in November.)

Name:

Work Space:

Answer:

_____

Daily Word Problems

Wednesday-Week 13

Weather

The following list shows the number of centimeters of snow that fell each day on Pikes Peak.

14 cm, 13 cm, 7 cm, 3 cm, 11 cm, 14 cm, 28 cm, 108 cm, 84 cm, 67 cm

What was the total snowfall for the 10 days listed?

Name:

Work Space:

Answer:

_____

Daily Word Problems

Thursday-Week 13

Weather

A weather map has a scale of 1 inch equals 10 miles. On the map, the distance from Tom's city to his cousin's town is 1 foot 3 inches. How many miles is it between the two cities?

Name:

Work Space:

Answer:

_____

Name:

Weather

Using the following circle graph, calculate the number of days during the month of October that were snowy, rainy, sunny, and cloudy. (Hint: There are 31 days in October.)

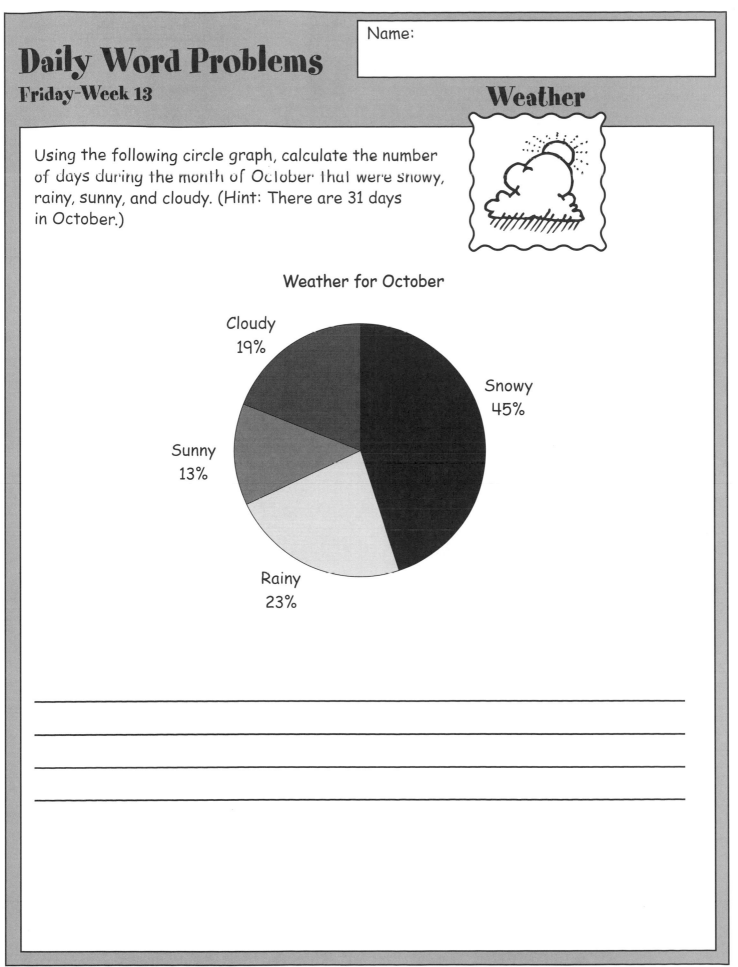

Weather for October

Cloudy
19%

Snowy
45%

Sunny
13%

Rainy
23%

_____

_____

_____

_____

Daily Word Problems

Monday–Week 14

Vending Machines

A vending machine sells each can of soda for $0.65. If 14 people bought sodas, how much money was deposited into the machine?

Name:

Work Space:

Answer:

_____

Daily Word Problems

Tuesday–Week 14

Vending Machines

Sally described the shape of a soda can as a cone. Sheryl described it as a cylinder. Draw a cone and a cylinder. Which shape should be used to describe a soda can?

Name:

Work Space:

Answer:

_____

Daily Word Problems

Wednesday-Week 14

Vending Machines

The candy machine in the bookstore has five rows to choose from with six items in each row. Currently, there are seven items that are sold out. If Ari randomly pushes a button, what is the probability he will select an item that is already sold out?

Name:

Work Space:

Answer:

_____

Daily Word Problems

Thursday-Week 14

Vending Machines

The vending machine requires exact change. Julianne wants to purchase some gum for 45¢. List **all** the different combinations of dimes and nickels she could use to purchase the gum.

Name:

Answer:

Daily Word Problems • EMC 3006

Name:

Vending Machines

The following figure represents a vending machine at Stephanie's school.

28 inches

5 feet

SODA

PUSH

$1\frac{1}{2}$ yards

- What is the volume of the vending machine in cubic inches?

_____

Daily Word Problems

Monday-Week 15

Bike Riding

Shelia rode her bike daily to get ready for a bike race. The following list shows the number of miles she rode each day of the week.

30, 27, 22, 32, 35, 18, 39

How many miles did Shelia average per week?

Name:

Work Space:

Answer:

_____

Daily Word Problems

Tuesday-Week 15

Bike Riding

Obed's bike is twice as heavy as Elsa's bike, but only 3 pounds heavier than George's bike. If George's bike weighs 15 pounds, how much does Elsa's bike weigh?

Name:

Work Space:

Answer:

_____

Daily Word Problems

Wednesday-Week 15

Bike Riding

The Great Bike Race had hundreds of competitors. The last competitor finished the race at 4:43 p.m. The range of the completion times was 2 hours and 36 minutes. Ty finished 4 minutes after the first place finisher. At what time did Ty cross the finish line?

Name:

Work Space:

Answer:

_____

Daily Word Problems

Thursday-Week 15

Bike Riding

A total of 453 people entered the Great Bike Race. All of the money from the entrance fees was being donated to cancer research. If the entrance fee was $28 for each participant, how much money was raised for cancer research?

Name:

Work Space:

Answer:

_____

Name:

Bike Riding

Use the clues below to determine who placed first, second, third, and fourth in the Great Bike Race.

When you know that a person and a place do **not** go with each other, make an X under the place and across from the person. When you know that a person and place do go together, write YES in that box. You can then X that person and place for all others.

Phil Martinez				
Susie Shelley				
Veronica Smith				
Carlos Cruz				

Clues:

1. Phil finished the race in third place.

2. The Shelley girl finished directly behind the Smith girl.

3. The person who finished in second place has the same first and last initials.

4. Carlos Cruz did not come in first place.

Daily Word Problems

Monday-Week 16

Card Games

Cara played a card game using a deck of 52 cards. After she dealt the same number of cards to 4 players, she had 24 cards left over. How many cards did each player get?

Name:

Work Space:

Answer:

_____

Daily Word Problems

Tuesday-Week 16

Card Games

Monique, Vic, and Ramon played a card game. Monique had one-third the number of points that Ramon had. Vic had one-half the points that Ramon had. If Ramon had 240 points, how many points did Monique and Vic have?

Name:

Work Space:

Answer:

_____

_____

Daily Word Problems

Wednesday-Week 16

Card Games

At the end of a card game, the loser divides his or her points evenly among the other players. When Steve lost, he had 3,248 points and had to divide them among the remaining 4 players. How many points did each player receive?

Name:

Work Space:

Answer:

_____

Daily Word Problems

Thursday-Week 16

Card Games

Yvonne had 23 points at the end of the first round of the game. At the end of the second round, her total score was -8. How many points did she lose during the second round?

Name:

Work Space:

Answer:

_____

Daily Word Problems

Friday-Week 16

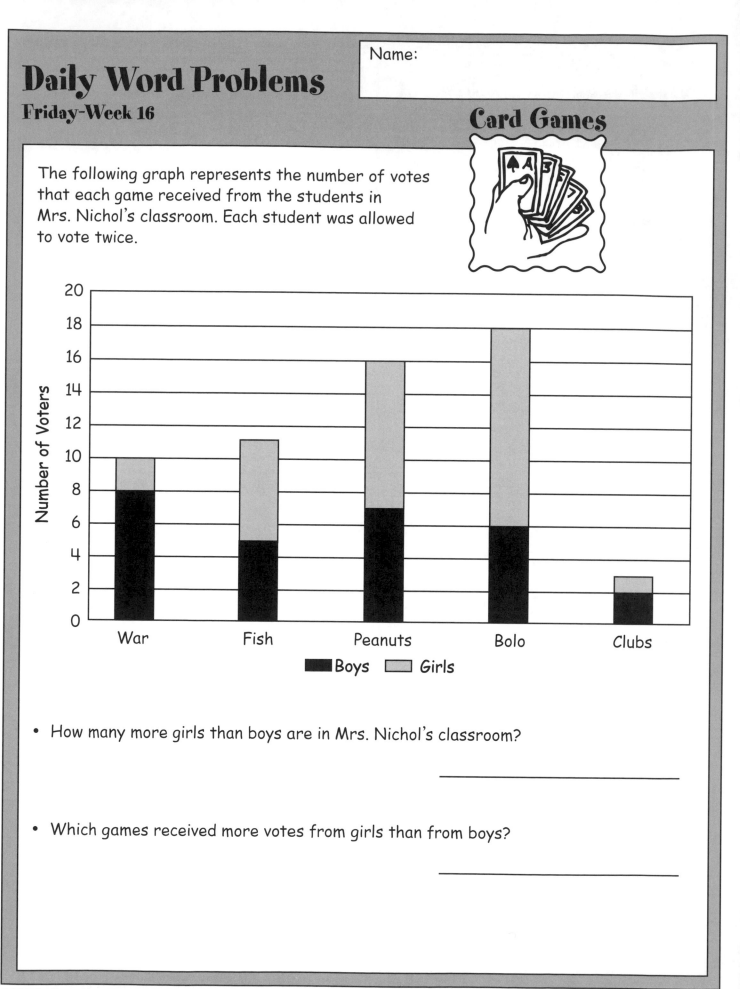

Name:

Card Games

The following graph represents the number of votes that each game received from the students in Mrs. Nichol's classroom. Each student was allowed to vote twice.

Number of Voters

20
18
16
14
12
10
8
6
4
2
0

War Fish Peanuts Bolo Clubs

■ Boys □ Girls

• How many more girls than boys are in Mrs. Nichol's classroom?

_____

• Which games received more votes from girls than from boys?

_____

Daily Word Problems

Monday–Week 17

Doctor's Appointments

Today there are 396 people scheduled for appointments and 12 doctors on duty at the clinic. How many patients should each doctor see in order to keep the number of appointments for each doctor as even as possible?

Name:

Work Space:

Answer:

_____

Daily Word Problems

Tuesday–Week 17

Doctor's Appointments

Andy's normal temperature is 98.6 degrees. Today his temperature is 101.2 degrees. How much higher than normal is his temperature?

Name:

Work Space:

Answer:

_____

Daily Word Problems

Wednesday-Week 17

Doctor's Appointments

A doctor used 20 inches of bandage material to wrap a patient's ankle. A roll of bandage material is 15 feet long. How much bandage material was left on the roll?

Name:

Work Space:

Answer:

Daily Word Problems

Thursday-Week 17

Doctor's Appointments

Gina arrived at 9:13 a.m. for her 9:30 a.m. appointment. She waited for 37 minutes before the nurse called her name. The nurse took Gina's weight, height, and temperature, which took 4 minutes. After that, she waited another 17 minutes before the doctor came in. At what time did the doctor enter her room?

Name:

Work Space:

Answer:

Daily Word Problems

Friday-Week 17

Name:

Doctor's Appointments

The following table lists the arrival times and the waiting times for six of the seven patients at Dr. Thompson's office.

Patient's Name	Arrival Time	Waiting Time
Tommy	9:06 a.m.	7 minutes
Amy	9:10 a.m.	11 minutes
April	9:11 a.m.	12 minutes
Peter	9:14 a.m.	4 minutes
Sharon	9:26 a.m.	10 minutes
Kiko	9:29 a.m.	11 minutes
Jerome	?	?

Use these clues to determine the arrival time and waiting time for Jerome.

1. The mode of the waiting times is 11 minutes.

2. The median of the waiting times is 10 minutes.

3. The mean of the waiting times is 9 minutes.

4. Jerome was called to see the doctor at 9:45.

_____   _____

Daily Word Problems

Monday-Week 18

Stamp Collection

My Stamp Collection

Rick and Myra collect stamps. Rick has 150 fewer stamps than Myra. Together they have collected 500 stamps. How many stamps does each person have in their collection?

Name:

Work Space:

Answer:

_____

_____

Daily Word Problems

Tuesday-Week 18

Stamp Collection

My Stamp Collection

Tomas bought a new sheet of stamps that had 10 thirty-four cent stamps on the page. If he paid with a ten-dollar bill, how much change did he get back?

Name:

Work Space:

Answer:

_____

Daily Word Problems

Wednesday-Week 18

Stamp Collection

Roberta keeps her stamp collection in a box that is 12 inches tall, 10 inches wide, and 3 inches deep. What three-dimensional geometric term can be used to describe the shape of her box?

Name:

Work Space:

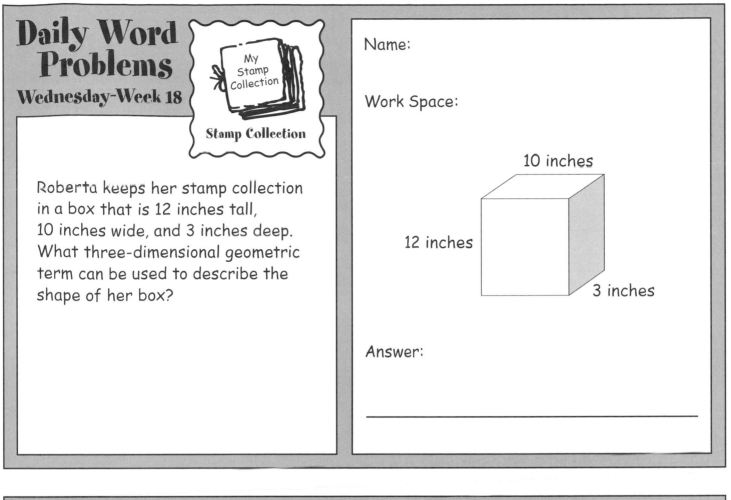

Answer:

_____

Daily Word Problems

Thursday-Week 18

Stamp Collection

Hugh has a stamp in his collection that his grandfather purchased for 24¢. The value of the stamp is now 300% of the original value. What is the current value of the stamp?

Name:

Work Space:

Answer:

_____

Daily Word Problems

Friday-Week 18

Stamp Collection

Erik, Jerry, Carol, and Sandy all collect stamps. They have their stamp collections stored in books that are different colors. Use the clues below to determine the color of each person's book and the number of stamps each book contains.

When you know that a person and a color or a person and a number of stamps do **not** go with each other, make an **X** under the color or number of stamps and across from the person. When you know that a person and color or a person and number of stamps do go together, write **YES** in that box.

	Black	Blue	Green	Red	315	720	1,205	2,403
Erik								
Jerry								
Carol								
Sandy								

Clues:

1. Carol has 1,205 stamps.

2. Sandy has the black book.

3. Neither Erik nor Jerry has the green book.

4. Erik has the red book.

5. The blue book contains the most stamps.

6. One of the boys (Erik or Jerry) has the fewest number of stamps and the other has the largest number of stamps.

Daily Word Problems • EMC 3006

Daily Word Problems

Monday-Week 19

Baby-sitting

Toby was baby-sitting a baby that weighed 264 ounces. How many pounds did the baby weigh? (Hint: One pound equals 16 ounces.)

Name:

Work Space:

Answer:

_____

Daily Word Problems

Tuesday-Week 19

Baby-sitting

For Parents' Night, several older kids offered to baby-sit young children in the school multipurpose room for 4 hours. They charged $2 per hour for the first child and $1 per hour for each additional child from the same family. The following list shows the number of children that were brought from 6 families.

3, 2, 5, 2, 3, 4

What was the total amount paid to the baby-sitters?

Name:

Work Space:

Answer:

_____

Daily Word Problems

Wednesday-Week 19

Baby-sitting

The Hernandez family has six baby-sitters whom they call regularly. Four of the baby-sitters are boys and two are girls. If they randomly call one of the baby-sitters, what is the chance that it will be a boy?

Name:

Work Space:

Answer:

_____

Daily Word Problems

Thursday-Week 19

Baby-sitting

The Roberts' twin boys play in a playpen with a base that measures 4 feet by 4 feet and a height of 2 feet. The floor has a good pad in it, but the netting on the four sides is rather worn and needs to be replaced. What is the area of the netting that they need to replace?

Name:

Work Space:

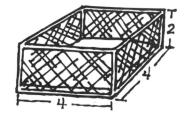

Answer:

_____

Daily Word Problems

Friday-Week 19

Baby-sitting

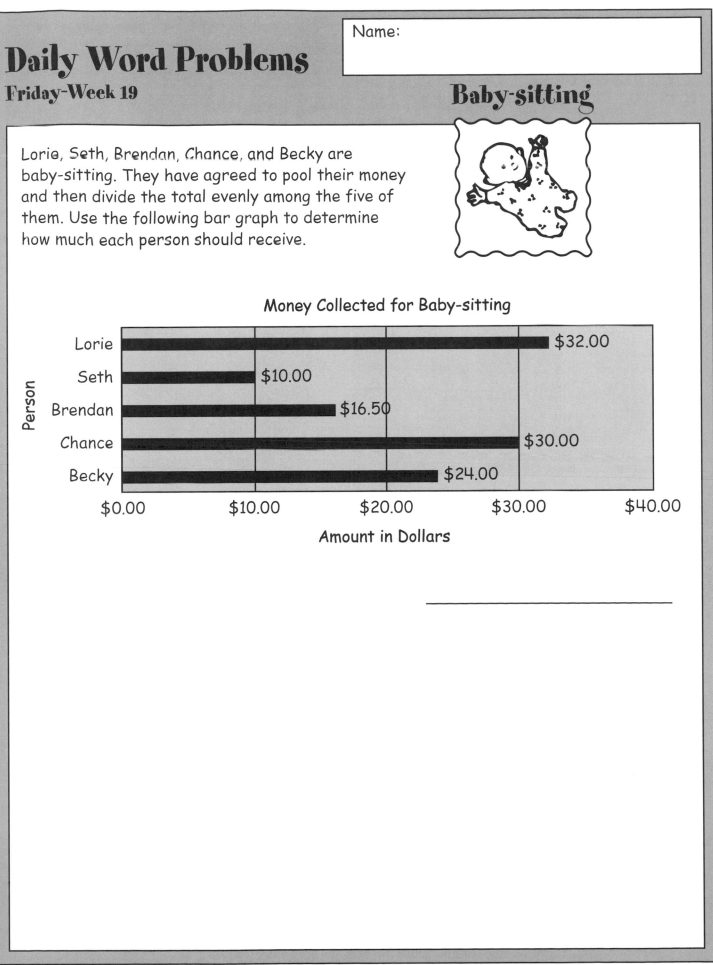

Lorie, Seth, Brendan, Chance, and Becky are baby-sitting. They have agreed to pool their money and then divide the total evenly among the five of them. Use the following bar graph to determine how much each person should receive.

Money Collected for Baby-sitting

Person

Lorie	$32.00
Seth	$10.00
Brendan	$16.50
Chance	$30.00
Becky	$24.00

$0.00 $10.00 $20.00 $30.00 $40.00

Amount in Dollars

_____

Daily Word Problems

Monday—Week 20

Baseball Card Collections

Jules purchased a box of baseball cards for her collection. The original price was $22.80, but the store was having a sale with $\frac{1}{4}$ off the price of all baseball cards. How much did the baseball cards cost with the discount?

Name:

Work Space:

Answer:

_____

Daily Word Problems

Tuesday—Week 20

Baseball Card Collections

In Mr. Layden's class, three students brought in their baseball card collections. For their three collections, the mode was 126 and the range was 26. What are two possibilities for the number of cards in each student's collection?

Name:

Work Space:

Answer:

_____

_____

Daily Word Problems

Wednesday-Week 20

Baseball Card Collections

Mr. Hurley collected baseball cards when his children were very young. Now that his children are older, he wants to give each of his three children the same number of cards to start their own collections. He has 3,732 cards. How many cards should each child receive?

Name:

Work Space:

Answer:

_____

Daily Word Problems

Thursday-Week 20

Baseball Card Collections

The kindergarten class has 432 baseball cards. They decided to lay the cards end-to-end down the hallway to see how far they would stretch. Each card is $3\frac{1}{2}$ inches long. How many feet long is the line of cards?

Name:

Work Space:

Answer:

_____

Name:

Baseball Card Collections

The following line graph represents the value of Jonathon's baseball card collection.

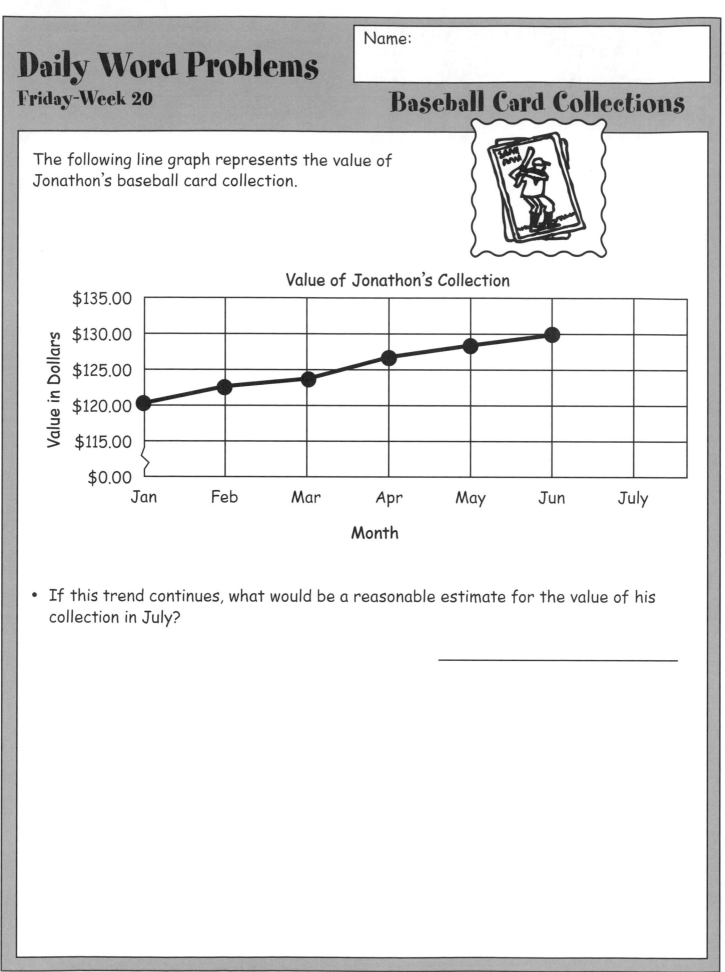

Value of Jonathon's Collection

- If this trend continues, what would be a reasonable estimate for the value of his collection in July?

_____

Daily Word Problems

Monday-Week 21

House Plants

Frank planted 200 tomato plants in a greenhouse. He plans to sell the plants this spring. How much should he sell each plant for if he wants to make a total of $150.00?

Name:

Work Space:

Answer:

_____

Daily Word Problems

Tuesday-Week 21

House Plants

Some of Helen's plants need water every day, some need water every other day, and others need water every third day. If she waters them all today, how many days will it be before she waters them all again?

Name:

Work Space:

Answer:

_____

Daily Word Problems

Wednesday-Week 21

House Plants

Saul bought several plants for the following prices: $2.97, $3, $3.50, $9.98, $5, and 79¢. What was the total cost of these plants?

Name:

Work Space:

Answer:

_____

Daily Word Problems

Thursday-Week 21

House Plants

Karen's watering can is in the shape of a cylinder. If the radius is 3 inches and the height is 10 inches, what is the volume of the can?

Hint: Volume of a cylinder = 3.14 x (radius)² x height

Name:

Work Space:

Answer:

_____

Daily Word Problems

Name: _____

House Plants

Use the clues below to determine the size of the pot for each plant.

Use the clues to help you fill in the names of the plants. When you know that a plant and a pot size do **not** go with each other, make an X under the pot size and across from the plant. When you know that a plant and pot size do go together, write YES in that box. You can then X that plant and pot size for all others.

	3 inch	4 inch	5 inch	6 inch	8 inch

Clues:

1. The geranium is planted in the smallest pot.

2. The sum of the spider plant's pot and the jade plant's pot is 14 inches.

3. The English ivy is planted in a pot with a prime number for its diameter.

4. The African violet is planted in a pot 2 inches smaller than the jade plant's pot.

Daily Word Problems

Monday-Week 22

Video Recordings

Gerald bought a videotape to record a basketball game. The videotape cost $3.55. If Gerald paid with a ten-dollar bill, what is the fewest number of bills and coins he could have received as change?

Name:

Work Space:

Answer:

_____

Daily Word Problems

Tuesday-Week 22

Video Recordings

James has four videotapes. Each one contains 120 minutes of recorded music videos. What is the total length of time recorded on all the videotapes?

Name:

Work Space:

Answer:

_____

Daily Word Problems

Wednesday–Week 22

Video Recordings

Stephanie went to the store and bought a new videotape. What is the geometric shape of a videocassette tape?

Name:

Work Space:

Answer:

_____

Daily Word Problems

Thursday–Week 22

Video Recordings

Alec had 24 videotapes. Brandon had half as many videotapes as Alec. Jason had half as many as Brandon. If each videotape has 90 minutes of recording time, how many hours of recording time do they have on all their videotapes?

Name:

Work Space:

Answer:

_____

Daily Word Problems

Friday-Week 22

Name:

Video Recordings

This chart represents the recording times of six music videos.

Song Number	Length of Song
One	3 minutes 38 seconds
Two	4 minutes 12 seconds
Three	3 minutes 48 seconds
Four	6 minutes 24 seconds
Five	5 minutes 8 seconds
Six	4 minutes 23 seconds

Troy would like to record all of these songs on a videotape that has 27 minutes left at the end. He would like to include a 5-second blank space between each of the songs. Does he have enough space to record all six songs? Explain your answer.

_____

_____

_____

Daily Word Problems

Monday-Week 23

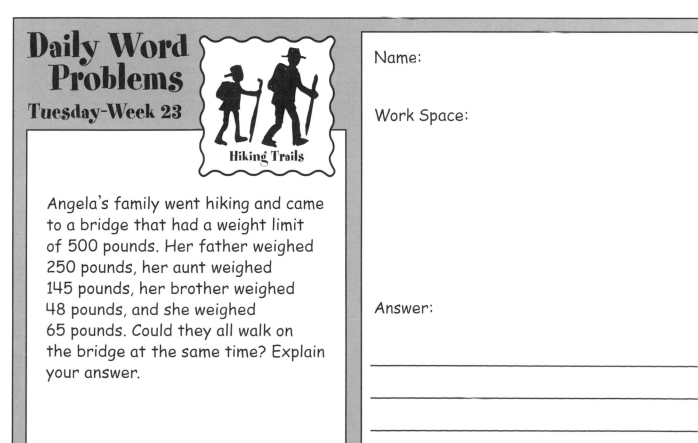

Hiking Trails

The scout troop placed 14 markers along a hiking trail. Each marker weighed 24 ounces. When they started out, they put them all in a large backpack that weighed 3 pounds. How much did the backpack weigh with all the markers?

Name:

Work Space:

Answer:

_____

Daily Word Problems

Tuesday-Week 23

Hiking Trails

Angela's family went hiking and came to a bridge that had a weight limit of 500 pounds. Her father weighed 250 pounds, her aunt weighed 145 pounds, her brother weighed 48 pounds, and she weighed 65 pounds. Could they all walk on the bridge at the same time? Explain your answer.

Name:

Work Space:

Answer:

_____

_____

_____

Daily Word Problems

Wednesday–Week 23

Hiking Trails

Jeff went on a long hike. He started out with a full canteen of water. During the first hour, he drank $\frac{1}{4}$ of the water. During the next hour, he drank $\frac{1}{2}$ of what was left. How full was his canteen at the end of the hike?

Name:

Work Space:

Answer:

_____

Daily Word Problems

Thursday–Week 23

Hiking Trails

Sean's family went on a hike. They kept a log of the changes in elevation each half hour. They started the hike at an elevation of 6,080 feet. The changes in elevation for the hike were +45, +200, -80, +35, -20, and +110. What was the elevation at the end of their hike?

Name:

Work Space:

Answer:

_____

Friday-Week 23

Hiking Trails

Name:

The following map represents different trails from the park entrance to Mountain Peak. List **all** the possible routes from the entrance to Mountain Peak without going on any trail more than once during a single route.

(Hint: There are 8 different routes.)

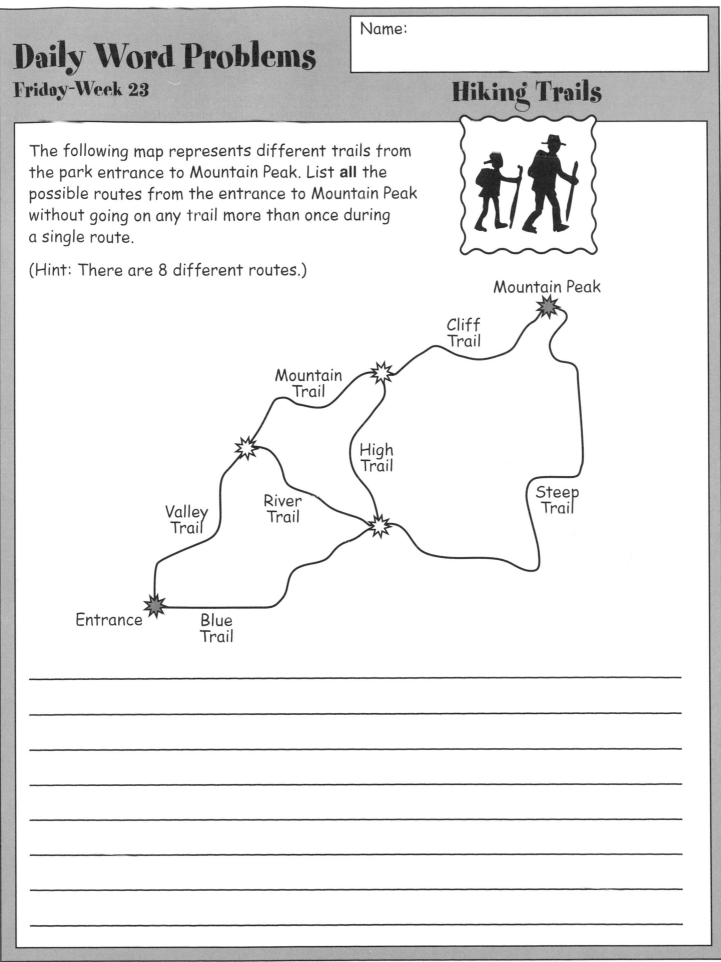

_____

_____

_____

_____

_____

_____

_____

_____

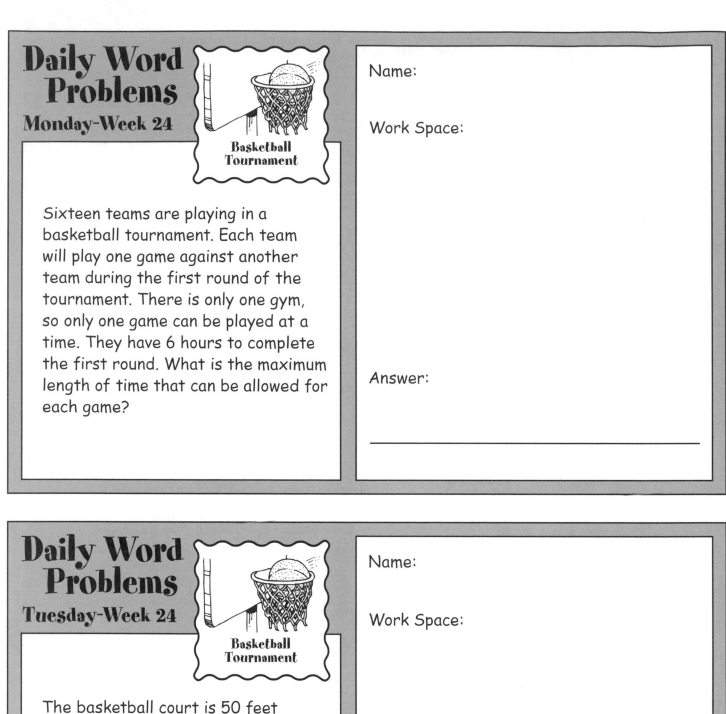

Daily Word Problems

Monday-Week 24

Basketball Tournament

Sixteen teams are playing in a basketball tournament. Each team will play one game against another team during the first round of the tournament. There is only one gym, so only one game can be played at a time. They have 6 hours to complete the first round. What is the maximum length of time that can be allowed for each game?

Name:

Work Space:

Answer:

_____

Daily Word Problems

Tuesday-Week 24

Basketball Tournament

The basketball court is 50 feet across by 94 feet long. There is a black line painted around the entire basketball court. What is the total area of the basketball court?

Name:

Work Space:

Answer:

_____

Daily Word Problems

Wednesday-Week 24

Basketball Tournament

The distance from the three-point line to the center of the basketball hoop is 19 feet 9 inches. What is the equivalent length in inches?

Name:

Work Space:

Answer:

_____

Daily Word Problems

Thursday-Week 24

Basketball Tournament

The first quarter of the championship game lasted 48 minutes. The second quarter lasted 52 minutes. There was a special presentation at halftime that lasted 25 minutes. The third quarter lasted 54 minutes and the fourth quarter lasted 49 minutes. If the game started at 6:30 p.m., at what time did the game finish?

Name:

Work Space:

Answer:

_____

Daily Word Problems

Basketball Tournament

Name:

Five middle schools played in an intramural basketball tournament. Use the clues below to determine how each school placed.

Use the clues to help you fill in the names of the schools and the places. When you know that a school and a place do **not** go with each other, make an X under the place and across from the school. When you know that a school and place do go together, write YES in that box. You can then X that school and place for all others.

Clues:

1. Franklin Middle School finished in third place.

2. Brentwood Middle School placed immediately after Franklin Middle School.

3. Central Middle School finished immediately ahead of West Middle School.

4. Heath Middle School placed directly after Brentwood Middle School.

5. Heath's place was the sum of Central's and Brentwood's places.

Daily Word Problems

Monday-Week 25

Baking Cookies

Shelley baked some cookies. She put 12 cookies on each cookie sheet. If she baked 24 cookie sheets of cookies, how many cookies did she bake in all?

Name:

Work Space:

Answer:

_____

Daily Word Problems

Tuesday-Week 25

Baking Cookies

Dave is decorating some cookies. He wants to buy three cans of frosting and two tubes of icing. Each can of frosting costs $0.79 and each tube of icing costs $1.29. How much will these items total?

Name:

Work Space:

Answer:

_____

Daily Word Problems • EMC 3006

Daily Word Problems

Wednesday-Week 25

Baking Cookies

Lance made 10 dozen cookies. He made 25% chocolate chip, 25% peanut butter, and the remaining 50% oatmeal raisin. How many of each type of cookie did he make?

Name:

Work Space:

Answer:

_____

_____

_____

Daily Word Problems

Thursday-Week 25

Baking Cookies

Andrea baked 250 cookies and wants to put them in bags of a dozen cookies each. How many full bags of cookies can she pack? How many cookies will be left over?

Name:

Work Space:

Answer:

_____

_____

Name:

Baking Cookies

The following chart shows the number of votes cast by the sixth-grade class for the students' favorite cookies.

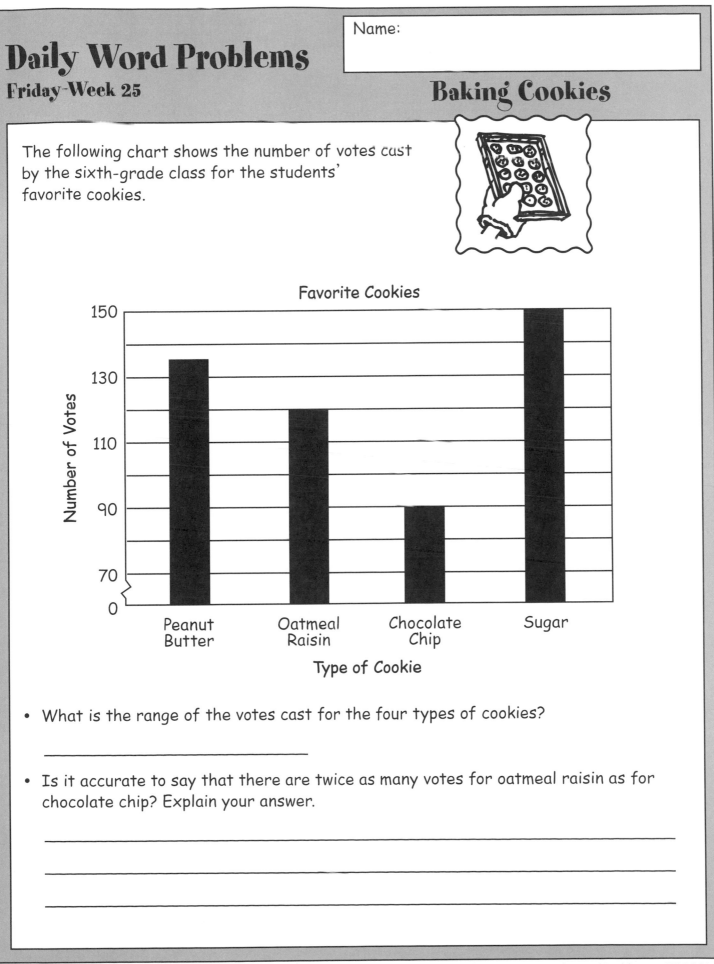

Favorite Cookies

- What is the range of the votes cast for the four types of cookies?

  _____

- Is it accurate to say that there are twice as many votes for oatmeal raisin as for chocolate chip? Explain your answer.

  _____

  _____

  _____

Daily Word Problems

Monday-Week 26

Library

Name:

Answer:

Derek's book is one day overdue and he must pay the overdue fine of 25¢. He has only nickels and pennies in his pocket. List three different combinations of nickels and pennies he can use to pay his fine.

Daily Word Problems

Tuesday-Week 26

Library

Name:

Work Space:

Kirk's books were due on October 14th. He didn't turn in his books until December 5th. How many days overdue were his library books?

Answer:

_____

Daily Word Problems

Wednesday-Week 26

Library

In the Greenwich Public Library, about one-tenth of the books are overdue when they are returned. An average of 580 books are returned to the library each day. About how many books could be expected to be returned on time each day?

Name:

Work Space:

Answer:

_____

Daily Word Problems

Thursday-Week 26

Library

In the center of the library is a fountain that holds 500 gallons of water. For every 25 gallons of water, they must add $\frac{1}{4}$ cup of water treatment. How many cups of water treatment must they add to the fountain to treat the 500 gallons of water?

Name:

Work Space:

Answer:

_____

Daily Word Problems

Name:

Library

There is a shelf in the library for the books by authors with the last names of Amster, Anderson, Axelson, Bannister, Baxter, and Bayer. The following table shows the number of books that the library has by these six authors and how many of those books are currently checked out.

Author's Last Name	Number of Books the Library Has	Number of Books Checked Out
Amster	8	2
Anderson	12	3
Axelson	1	0
Bannister	5	2
Baxter	4	1
Bayer	7	1

• If Robert randomly selects one book from the remaining books on the shelf, what is the probability that the author of the book he selects will be Baxter?

_____

Daily Word Problems

Monday-Week 27

Spelling Bee

There were 350 students competing at the regional spelling bee. During the first round, 20% of the contestants were eliminated. How many contestants were still in the competition at the beginning of the second round?

Name:

Work Space:

Answer:

_____

Daily Word Problems

Tuesday-Week 27

Spelling Bee

At the state spelling bee, there were 120 students. One-fourth of the students were eliminated during the first round. One-third of the remaining students were eliminated during the second round. Two-thirds of the remaining students were eliminated during the third round. How many students were left after the third round?

Name:

Work Space:

Answer:

_____

Daily Word Problems

Wednesday-Week 27

Spelling Bee

The average length of the eight words Betty was asked to spell was 9 letters. The first seven words had the following lengths: 8 letters, 9 letters, 6 letters, 10 letters, 7 letters, 9 letters, and 11 letters. What was the length of the eighth word?

Name:

Work Space:

Answer:

_____

Daily Word Problems

Thursday-Week 27

Spelling Bee

A total of $924 was collected in registration fees. In addition, another $527 was collected at the concession stand. The costs for the day totaled $895. After subtracting the total costs from the total money collected, how much money was left?

Name:

Work Space:

Answer:

_____

Name:

Spelling Bee

The following figure represents the stage area where the spelling bee was held.

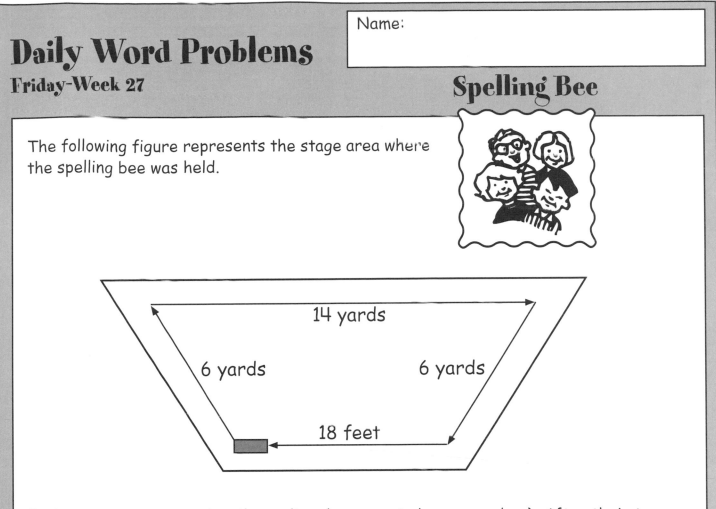

Each contestant started at the podium (represented as a gray box). After their turn, they followed the arrows around the stage in a line until it was their turn again. Kelly was the first in line for the first round. When Kelly stood at the podium for her fifth word, how far had she walked around the staging area?

_____

Daily Word Problems

Monday-Week 28

Food Drive

Each food item contributed to the local food bank is recorded as a positive number, while each food item donated to a family is recorded as a negative number. The food bank started with 508 items. How many items were on the shelves after the following contributions and donations?

–8, –29, +17, –12, –9

Name:

Work Space:

Answer:

_____

Daily Word Problems

Tuesday-Week 28

Food Drive

Jason's family donated 12 cases of soup for the school's food drive. Each case had four rows with six cans of soup in each row. How many cans of soup did Jason's family donate in all?

Name:

Work Space:

Answer:

_____

Daily Word Problems

Wednesday–Week 28

Food Drive

Scott School collected 2,970 cans of food during their food drive. If they can put 35 cans in each box, how many boxes will they need for all the food?

Name:

Work Space:

Answer:

_____

Daily Word Problems

Thursday–Week 28

Food Drive

For every can of corn that was donated at Tia's school, 1.2 cans of green beans were donated. If there were 590 cans of corn donated, how many cans of green beans were donated?

Name:

Work Space:

Answer:

_____

Daily Word Problems

Friday-Week 28

Food Drive

Five sixth-grade classes collected canned food for the local food bank. Each class collected a different number of cans. Use the following clues to determine how many cans were collected in each class.

1. The five classes that collected cans include two classes with totals in the three hundreds, two classes with totals in the four hundreds, and one class with a total in the five hundreds.

2. The smallest total was 308 cans.

3. The range of the total cans collected was 262.

4. The median number of cans collected was 421.

5. The total of the two classes in the three hundreds was 706.

6. The total number of cans collected from all the classes was 2,130.

_____

Daily Word Problems
Monday-Week 29

Baseball

A baseball diamond is formed by placing four bases 90 feet apart at each corner of the infield. If each corner of the infield forms a 90-degree angle, what shape is a baseball diamond?

Name:

Work Space:

Answer:

_____

Daily Word Problems
Tuesday-Week 29

Baseball

Shawn was at bat 20 times during the last game. He hit the ball one-fourth of the times that he was at bat. How many times did he hit the ball?

Name:

Work Space:

Answer:

_____

Daily Word Problems

Wednesday-Week 29

Baseball

There are 14 boys and 15 girls in Mr. Bell's class playing baseball. If he randomly pulls a name out of a hat to determine who will bat first, what is the probability that Kevin will bat first?

Name:

Work Space:

Answer:

_____

Daily Word Problems

Thursday-Week 29

Baseball

On a baseball diamond there are 90 feet between each of the four bases. When Calesha runs, she travels about one yard for each step. About how many steps does she take to go around the baseball diamond?

Name:

Work Space:

Answer:

_____

Daily Word Problems

Name: _____

Baseball

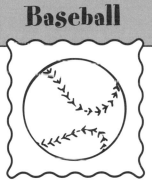

The following table lists the batting averages of five players.

Player's Name	Batting Average
Ralph	0.263
Antonio	0.125
Elisa	0.300
Teresa	0.248
Marcos	0.150

A batting average of 0.500 means that the batter hits the ball 50% of the times he or she is at bat.

• Which of the players has the highest batting average?

_____

• What percent of the times at bat did that player hit the ball?

_____

         Daily Word Problems • EMC 3006

Daily Word Problems

Monday-Week 30

Movie Theater

The Fox movie theater has 360 seats. There are 500 students in the sixth grade. If 80% of the sixth-grade students want to go to the Fox theater for a class fieldtrip, will there be enough seats for all the students?

Name:

Work Space:

Answer:

_____

Daily Word Problems

Tuesday-Week 30

Movie Theater

When Marissa's family entered the Galaxy movie theater, 45% of the 600 seats were filled. How many people were already in the theater?

Name:

Work Space:

Answer:

_____

Daily Word Problems

Wednesday-Week 30

Movie Theater

At the movie theater, Celeste bought 2 large drinks and 2 large popcorns for $8.50. She paid with a twenty-dollar bill. What is the fewest number of bills and coins that she could have received as change?

Name:

Work Space:

Answer:

_____

Daily Word Problems

Thursday-Week 30

Movie Theater

The Chavez family was seated in the movie theater at 6:53 p.m. Eight minutes later, 12 minutes of movie previews were shown before the movie finally started. The movie finished at 9:27 p.m. How long was the movie?

Name:

Work Space:

Answer:

_____

Daily Word Problems

Name:

Movie Theater

Cinema 8 shows a different movie in each of its eight theaters. The wind blew some of the letters off the sign that shows which movie is shown in which theater.

1	t	o	5	te	we
2	h	pp	6	t	eet
3	e	e	7	W	ea
4	it	oerp	8	i	ow

Natasha and her friends wanted to see the movie entitled *White Tower*. They looked at the sign and tried to figure out which titles could possibly be *White Tower*. Then they picked one of those possibilities at random. What is the probability that they picked the theater that was actually showing *White Tower*? Explain your answer.

_____

_____

_____

_____

Daily Word Problems

Monday-Week 31

Auction Today

Auction

There was a fish tank for sale at the City Auction. At the beginning of the auction it had 10 gallons of water in it. Thirty minutes later, 1 cup of water had leaked out. How much water was left in the tank? (Hint: There are 4 cups in a quart and 4 quarts in a gallon.)

Name:

Work Space:

Answer:

_____

Daily Word Problems

Tuesday-Week 31

Auction Today

Auction

Caleb purchased several items at the auction. He bought a new bike for $85, a television for $45, a desk for $80, and a computer for $225. How much did he spend in all?

Name:

Work Space:

Answer:

_____

Daily Word Problems

Wednesday-Week 31

Auction Today

Auction

At the auction last week, there were 16,887 baseball cards in several boxes for sale. Three people got together to buy all of the baseball cards. If they divided the cards equally among themselves, how many cards would each person get?

Name:

Work Space:

Answer:

_____

Daily Word Problems

Thursday-Week 31

Auction Today

Auction

The seats at the auction were each 0.47 meters wide. If there were 12 seats in each row, how long was each row in meters? (Assume that there was no space between the seats.)

Name:

Work Space:

Answer:

_____

Name:

Auction

Craig went to an auction and bought five different items. Use the clues below to determine the price he paid for each item.

Use the clues to help you fill in the items and the prices. When you know that an item and a price do **not** go with each other, make an **X** under the price and across from the item. When you know that an item and a price do go together, write **YES** in that box. You can then **X** that item and price for all others.

Clues:

1. The chair was the most expensive item, which sold for $95.

2. The range of the prices of the five items was $75.

3. The stereo was the least expensive item.

4. Craig bought the TV for $25.

5. The video game player was $20 more than the TV.

6. The bed was $60 more than the stereo.

Daily Word Problems

Monday-Week 32

Hot Dog Vendor

Clarence wants to buy six hot dogs for himself and his two friends to share. If each hot dog costs $1.40, how much will six hot dogs cost?

Name:

Work Space:

Answer:

_____

Daily Word Problems

Tuesday-Week 32

Hot Dog Vendor

A one-pound package of hot dogs contains 8 hot dogs. If the vendor has room for 90 hot dogs in his warmer, what is the greatest number of full packages that will fit in the warmer?

Name:

Work Space:

Answer:

_____

Daily Word Problems

Wednesday-Week 32

Hot Dog Vendor

Louis wants to buy a hot dog for $1.40, a drink for $1.70, and a bag of chips for $1.30. If he gets $\frac{1}{4}$ off his total purchase, how much will all three items cost?

Name:

Work Space:

Answer:

_____

Daily Word Problems

Thursday-Week 32

Hot Dog Vendor

The hot dog vendor is purchasing hot dog buns. The buns come in packages of 12. He sells an average of 130 hot dogs a day. If he purchases buns for three days at a time, how many packages should he get?

Name:

Work Space:

Answer:

_____

Daily Word Problems

Friday-Week 32

Hot Dog Vendor

The following graph represents the number of hot dogs that were sold on each day of the week.

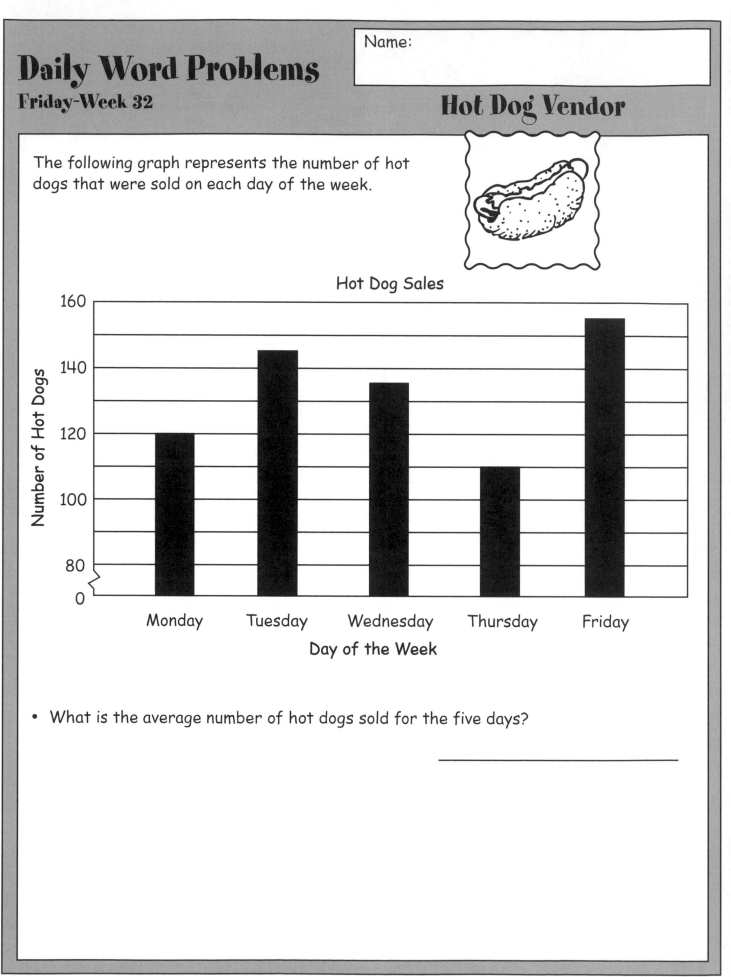

Hot Dog Sales

- What is the average number of hot dogs sold for the five days?

_____

Daily Word Problems

Monday-Week 33

Fundraising

Mrs. Garcia's class wants to raise money for some new playground equipment. A slide costs $240.00, a swing set costs $300.00, and a climbing set will cost $1,680.00. What is the total cost of all the playground equipment?

Name:

Work Space:

Answer:

_____

Daily Word Problems

Tuesday-Week 33

Fundraising

The big slide that the students want to order is 4 yards tall. The swing set is 14 feet tall. The climbing set is 156 inches tall. Which piece of equipment is the tallest?

Name:

Work Space:

Answer:

_____

Daily Word Problems

Wednesday-Week 33

Fundraising

The students in Mrs. Garcia's class will sell magazine subscriptions to raise money for the new playground equipment. The statistics from the magazine company show that one out of every 5 people asked will buy a subscription. Based on the company's statistics, if Marcia asks 355 people, how many subscriptions could she expect to sell?

Name:

Work Space:

Answer:

_____

Daily Word Problems

Thursday-Week 33

Fundraising

Mrs. Garcia has twenty students in her class. The following list shows the number of subscriptions each student sold.

11, 9, 7, 12, 41, 37, 18, 10, 11, 13, 15, 37, 11, 13, 1, 32, 11, 25, 19, 27

What is the median, the mode, and the range for the subscriptions sold?

Name:

Work Space:

Answer:

_____

_____

_____

The class earned $5 for every subscription sold for *Fishing Magazine,* $10 for every subscription sold for *Auto Repair Monthly,* $4 for every subscription sold for *Home Lifestyle Magazine,* and $6 for every subscription sold for *Kids Weekly.*

The following chart shows the number of subscriptions sold for each magazine.

Magazine	Number of Subscriptions Sold
Fishing Magazine	65
Auto Repair Monthly	95
Home Lifestyle Magazine	92
Kids Weekly	108

- Based on the subscription totals given, did the class earn enough money to purchase $2,220 worth of playground equipment? Explain your answer.

_____

_____

_____

Daily Word Problems

Monday-Week 34

Fishing

Maurice went fishing with his dad and his brother. His dad caught a fish that weighed 2 pounds 4 ounces. Maurice's brother's fish weighed 6 ounces less than his dad's fish. Maurice caught a fish that weighed twice as much as his brother's fish. How much did Maurice's fish weigh?

Name:

Work Space:

Answer:

_____

Daily Word Problems

Tuesday-Week 34

Fishing

Vonni went fishing with her father and caught a fish that was 31 inches less than twice the length of her dad's fish. Her dad's fish was half a yard in length. How long was Vonni's fish?

Name:

Work Space:

Answer:

_____

Daily Word Problems

Wednesday-Week 34

Fishing

Charity and her family went fishing. They put their minnows in a rectangular container that was 20 centimeters by 12 centimeters by 15 centimeters. What was the volume of the container?

Name:

Work Space:

Answer:

_____

Daily Word Problems

Thursday-Week 34

Fishing

The city stocked West Lake with 455 fish. If they allow a total of 27 fish to be caught each day, how many days will it take for all the fish to be caught?

Name:

Work Space:

Answer:

_____

Daily Word Problems

Friday-Week 34

Fishing

Jordan, Marybeth, Meredith, Taylor, and Scott all went fishing. They each caught one fish. Use the clues below to determine the length of each person's fish.

Use the clues to help you fill in the length of each fish and the person who caught it. When you know that a person and a length do **not** go with each other, make an **X** under the length and across from the person. When you know that a person and length do go together, write **YES** in that box. You can then **X** that person and length for all others.

Clues:

1. The mode of the lengths was 10 inches. This was also the median value of the five fish.

2. The longest fish was 12 inches.

3. Three of the lengths are consecutive even numbers starting with 8 inches.

4. The range of the lengths of the fish was 7 inches.

5. Scott caught the smallest fish.

6. Meredith and Marybeth were the only ones to catch fish that were the same length.

7. Jordan's fish was 4 inches shorter than Taylor's fish.

Daily Word Problems • EMC 3006

Daily Word Problems

Monday–Week 35

CD Collections

Jeremy and Todd are looking at the shape of a CD. Jeremy says that CDs are shaped like a circle. Todd says that CDs are shaped like a cylinder. Which geometric term describes the shape of a CD? Explain why.

Name:

Work Space:

Answer:

_____

_____

_____

Daily Word Problems

Tuesday–Week 35

CD Collections

Ginny prefers to buy CDs in sets of six. If she has 138 CDs from these sets, how many sets does she have?

Name:

Work Space:

Answer:

_____

Daily Word Problems

Wednesday·Week 35

CD Collections

Isaac has been saving his allowance to buy three CDs. Each CD costs $14.98. What will be the total for the CDs?

Name:

Work Space:

Answer:

_____

Daily Word Problems

Thursday·Week 35

CD Collections

Gabriela is listening to her new CD. The time for each song is listed below.

    4 minutes 22 seconds
    5 minutes 11 seconds
    3 minutes 26 seconds
    9 minutes 58 seconds
    7 minutes   3 seconds

If she starts listening to the CD at 3:45 in the afternoon, at what time will the CD end?

Name:

Work Space:

Answer:

_____

Name:

CD Collections

The following graph represents the portion of the CD that each song uses.

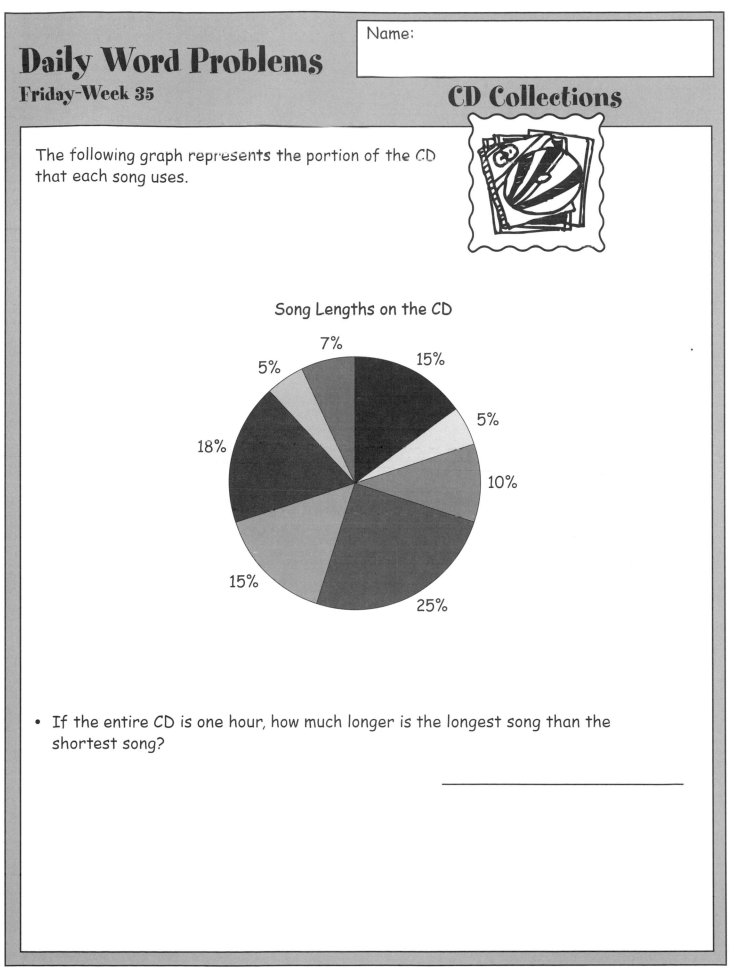

Song Lengths on the CD

7%
5%
15%
5%
18%
10%
15%
25%

- If the entire CD is one hour, how much longer is the longest song than the shortest song?

_____

Daily Word Problems

Monday–Week 36

Vacations

There are 30 students in Mr. Call's class. One-third of the students are traveling somewhere this summer vacation. Of those traveling, one-fifth are going out of the country. How many students are traveling out of the country?

Name: _____

Work Space:

Answer:

_____

Daily Word Problems

Tuesday–Week 36

Vacations

During summer vacation, Ricky is planning to take his fourteen cousins to a water park near his house. The entrance fee for the park is $24. How much will it cost for all of them to get into the water park?

Name: _____

Work Space:

Answer:

_____

Daily Word Problems

Wednesday-Week 36

Vacations

Last year Park Summer Camp had 520 campers in grades 6 through 8. The projected enrollment for this year compared to last year will be +29 campers in sixth grade, -53 campers in seventh grade, and +16 campers in eighth grade. What is the total expected enrollment for this year?

Name:

Work Space:

Answer:

_____

Daily Word Problems

Thursday-Week 36

Vacations

Alf is saving money to take on his trip this summer. He has 15 one-dollar bills and 5 five-dollar bills. He also has 83 quarters, 90 dimes, 120 nickels, and 208 pennies. How much money has he saved for his summer trip?

Name:

Work Space:

Answer:

_____

Daily Word Problems

Friday-Week 36

Vacations

Wade, Kira, Roslyn, and Ryan each plan to take a family trip to a different state, each during a different month (June, July, August, and September). Use the clues below to determine to what state and in what month each person will travel.

When you know that a person and a state or a person and a month do **not** go with each other, make an **X** under the state or month and across from the person. When you know that a person and a state or a person and a month do go together, write **YES** in that box.

Clues:

1. Kira's family is not planning a trip to Arkansas or Montana.

2. Wade is going on his family trip during the month of August.

3. One of the boys is going to Washington.

4. The family that is going to Montana is traveling during the month of August.

5. Kira's family is traveling to South Dakota the month immediately after Ryan's family.

Answer Key

Week 1
Monday—224 swimmers
Tuesday—78.1 degrees
Wednesday—800 meters
Thursday—1 minute 47 seconds
Friday—Susan-second, Janice-fourth, Maria-fifth,
    Jennifer-first, Emily-third

Week 2
Monday—8:00 a.m.
Tuesday—2 bills and 1 coin (1 $5 bill,
    1 $1 bill, and 1 50¢ piece)
Wednesday—$1.50
Thursday—6 cups; 1½ quarts OR 1 quart 2 cups
Friday—$4.47

Week 3
Monday—18 adults
Tuesday—2/5
Wednesday—$5.25
Thursday—14,000 pounds
Friday—1,680 square feet

Week 4
Monday—¼ cup
Tuesday—8 rectangles
Wednesday—88 fish
Thursday—276 fish
Friday—$300.00

Week 5
Monday—$10.50
Tuesday—1,051 people
Wednesday—23 feet 11 inches
Thursday—Any 3 of the following combinations:
    2 dimes and 1 penny; 1 dime, 2 nickels, and 1 penny;
    1 dime, 1 nickel, and 6 pennies; 4 nickels and
    1 penny; 3 nickels and 6 pennies; 2 nickels and
    11 pennies; 1 nickel and 16 pennies; 21 pennies
Friday—Daniel-11, Dwight-13, Janet-14, Harry-10,
    Suzy-12

Week 6
Monday—24 students
Tuesday—7:05 a.m.
Wednesday—$104
Thursday—91 buses
Friday—Evans to Grover to LaSalle to Westview
    (102 minutes)

Week 7
Monday—$124
Tuesday—25 pounds under the maximum weight
Wednesday—6 ways
Thursday—$3.00
Friday—166 feet; Yes, you can add one length
    of the shop (55 feet) and one width of the
    shop (28 feet) and then double it.

Week 8
Monday—312 feet
Tuesday—3 cups
Wednesday—625 forks
Thursday—126 people
Friday—Station 1-$206, Station 2-$255,
    Station 3-$343, Station 4-$112

Week 9
Monday—$9.98
Tuesday—768 boxes
Wednesday—rectangular prism; rectangle
Thursday—19 pennies; 1 nickel and 14 pennies;
    2 nickels and 9 pennies; 1 dime and 9 pennies;
    3 nickels and 4 pennies; 1 dime, 1 nickel, and
    4 pennies
Friday—$3,074.96

Week 10
Monday—528 miles
Tuesday—28 minutes 10.82 seconds
Wednesday—$49,200
Thursday—2,090 empty seats
Friday—Range is 48 seconds; average is
    4 minutes 48 seconds

Week 11
Monday—$84.50
Tuesday—5:30 p.m.
Wednesday—1/8
Thursday—31 pieces of candy, 1 piece left over
Friday—There are many possible answers including:
    6:04 p.m.-He turned the faucet off; 6:09 p.m.-He
    turned the faucet on; 6:14 p.m.-He turned the
    faucet off and opened the drain.

Week 12
Monday—½ cup of brown sugar; 3 cups of white sugar
Tuesday—3 sticks of butter, ¾ pound
Wednesday—24 cookies
Thursday—No change
Friday—Bryan-peach pie, Jose-apple pie,
    Linda-chocolate pie, Nan-cherry pie,
    Victor-pecan pie

Week 13
Monday— ⁻6 degrees OR 6 degrees below zero
Tuesday—6 days
Wednesday—349 centimeters
Thursday—150 miles
Friday—14 snowy, 7 rainy, 4 sunny, 6 cloudy

Week 14
Monday—$9.10
Tuesday—(cone) (cylinder); cylinder
    A can of soda is a cylinder.
Wednesday—7/30
Thursday—4 dimes and 1 nickel; 3 dimes and 3 nickels;
    2 dimes and 5 nickels; 1 dime and 7 nickels;
    9 nickels
Friday—90,720 cubic inches

Week 15
Monday—29 miles
Tuesday—9 pounds
Wednesday—2:11 p.m.
Thursday—$12,684
Friday—Phil Martinez-third, Susie Shelley-second,
    Veronica Smith-first, Carlos Cruz-fourth

Week 16
Monday—7 cards
Tuesday—Monique had 80 points; Vic had
    120 points
Wednesday—812 points
Thursday—lost 31 points
Friday—1 more girl; Fish, Peanuts, and Bolo

Week 17
Monday—33 patients
Tuesday—2.6 degrees higher
Wednesday—13 feet 4 inches
Thursday—10:11 a.m.
Friday—Arrival time is 9:37 a.m.; waiting time is
    8 minutes

Week 18
Monday—Rick has 175 stamps, Myra has 325 stamps
Tuesday—$6.60
Wednesday—Prism OR rectangular prism
Thursday—72¢
Friday—Erik has 315 stamps in a red book,
    Jerry has 2403 stamps in a blue book, Carol
    has 1205 stamps in a green book, Sandy has
    720 stamps in a black book.

Week 19
Monday—16½ pounds
Tuesday—$100
Wednesday—4/6 OR 2/3
Thursday—32 square feet
Friday—$22.50

Week 20
Monday—$17.10
Tuesday—100, 126, 126; 126, 126, 152
Wednesday—1,244 cards
Thursday—126 feet
Friday—Answers will vary, but should be
    around $132.00.

Week 21
Monday—75¢ each
Tuesday—6 days
Wednesday—$25.24
Thursday—282.6 cubic inches
Friday—3 inch geranium, 4 inch African violet,
    5 inch English ivy, 6 inch jade plant,
    8 inch spider plant

Week 22
Monday—5 bills and coins (1 $5 bill, 1 $1 bill,
    1 quarter, and 2 dimes)
Tuesday—8 hours OR 480 minutes
Wednesday—rectangular prism
Thursday—63 hours
Friday—No, the length of time needed is 27 minutes
    58 seconds, which is 58 seconds too long.

Week 23
Monday—24 pounds
Tuesday—No, they are over the maximum weight by
    8 pounds.
Wednesday—3/8 full
Thursday—6,370 feet
Friday—Valley to Mountain to Cliff; Valley to Mountain
    to High to Steep; Valley to River to High to Cliff;
    Valley to River to Steep; Blue to River to Mountain
    to Cliff; Blue to River to Mountain to High to
    Steep; Blue to High to Cliff; Blue to Steep

Week 24
Monday—45 minutes
Tuesday—4,700 square feet
Wednesday—237 inches
Thursday—10:18 p.m.
Friday—Central is first, West is second, Franklin is
    third, Brentwood is fourth, Heath is fifth.

Week 25
Monday—288 cookies
Tuesday—$4.95
Wednesday—30 chocolate chip, 30 peanut butter,
    and 60 oatmeal raisin
Thursday—20 full bags, 10 cookies left over
Friday—The range is 60 votes; No, the bar looks
    twice as long because the vertical axis goes from
    0 to 70 in the first interval.

Week 26
Monday—Any three of the following: 5 nickels;
    4 nickels and 5 pennies; 3 nickels and 10 pennies;
    2 nickels and 15 pennies; 1 nickel and 20 pennies;
    25 pennies
Tuesday—52 days
Wednesday—About 522 books
Thursday—5 cups
Friday—3 out of 28 OR 3/28

Week 27
Monday—280 contestants
Tuesday—20 students
Wednesday—12 letters
Thursday—$556
Friday—384 feet OR 128 yards

Week 28
Monday—467 items
Tuesday—288 cans
Wednesday—85 boxes
Thursday—708 cans
Friday—308, 398, 421, 433, and 570 cans

Week 29
Monday—square
Tuesday—5 times
Wednesday—1 out of 29 OR 1/29
Thursday—About 120 steps
Friday—Elisa; 30%